Mapping Eastleigh for Christian-Muslim Relations

Zapf Chancery Tertiary Level Publications

A Guide to Academic Writing by C. B. Peter (1994)
Africa in the 21st Century by Eric M. Aseka (1996)
Women in Development by Egara Kabaji (1997)
Introducing Social Science: A Guidebook by J. H. van Doorne (2000)
Elementary Statistics by J. H. van Doorne (2001)
Iteso Survival Rites on the Birth of Twins by Festus B. Omusolo (2001)
The Church in the New Millennium: Three Studies in the Acts of the Apostles by John Stott (2002)
Introduction to Philosophy in an African Perspective by Cletus N. Chukwu (2002)
Participatory Monitoring and Evaluation by Francis W. Mulwa and Simon N. Nguluu (2003)
Applied Ethics and HIV/AIDS in Africa by Cletus N. Chukwu (2003)
For God and Humanity: 100 Years of St. Paul's United Theological College Edited by Emily Onyango (2003)
Establishing and Managing School Libraries and Resource Centres by Margaret Makenzi and Raymond Ongus (2003)
Introduction to the Study of Religion by Nehemiah Nyaundi (2003)
A Guest in God's World: Memories of Madagascar by Patricia McGregor (2004)
Introduction to Critical Thinking by J. Kahiga Kiruki (2004)
Theological Education in Contemporary Africa edited by Grant LeMarquand and Joseph D. Galgalo (2004)
Looking Religion in the Eye edited by Kennedy Onkware (2004)
Computer Programming: Theory and Practice by Gerald Injendi (2005)
Demystifying Participatory Development by Francis W. Mulwa (2005)
Music Education in Kenya: A Historical Perspective by Hellen A. Odwar (2005)
Into the Sunshine: Integrating HIV/AIDS into Ethics Curriculum Edited by Charles Klagba and C. B. Peter (2005)
Integrating HIV/AIDS into Ethics Curriculum: Suggested Modules Edited by Charles Klagba (2005)
Dying Voice (An Anthropological Novel) by Andrew K. Tanui (2006)
Participatory Learning and Action (PLA): A Guide to Best Practice by Enoch Harun Opuka (2006)
Science and Human Values: Essays in Science, Religion, and Modern Ethical Issues edited by Nehemiah Nyaundi and Kennedy Onkware (2006)
Understanding Adolescent Behaviour by Daniel Kasomo (2006)
Students' Handbook for Guidance and Counseling by Daniel Kasomo (2007)
Business Organization and Management: Questions and Answers by Musa O. Nyakora (2007)
Auditing Principles: A Students' Handbook by Musa O. Nyakora (2007)
The Concept of Botho *and HIV/AIDS in Botswana* edited by Joseph B. R. Gaie and Sana K. MMolai (2007)
Captive of Fate: A Novel by Ketty Arucy (2007)
A Guide to Ethics by Joseph Njino (2008)
Pastoral Theology: Rediscovering African Models and Methods by John N. B. Ikenye (2009)
The Royal Son: Balancing Barthian and African Christologies by Zablon Bundi Mutongu (2009)
AIDS, Sexuality, and Gender: Experiences of Women in Kenyan Universities by Nyokabi Kamau (2009)
Modern Facilitation and Training and Training Methodology: A Guide to Best Practice in Africa by Frederick Chelule (2009)
How to Write a Winning Thesis by Simon Kang'ethe et al (2009)
Absolute Power and Other Stories by Ambrose Rotich Keitany (2009)
Y'sdom in Africa: A Personal Journey by Stanley Kinyeki (2010)

Mapping Eastleigh for Christian-Muslim Relations

Edited by
C. B. Peter
Joseph Wandera
Willem J. E. Jansen

**Zapf Chancery Publishers Africa Ltd
Limuru, Kenya**

First Published 2013
© Authors
All rights reserved.

Cover Concept and Design
Willem J. E. Jansen and C. B. Peter

Copyediting
Kirsten Krymusa

Editors
C. B. Peter, Joseph Wandera, and Willem J. E. Jansen

Printed by
Kijabe Printing Press,
P. O. Box 40,
Kijabe.

Published by

Zapf Chancery Publishers Africa Ltd
C/O St. Paul's University
Private Bag
Limuru 00217, Kenya
Email: info@zapfchancery.org
Website: www.zapfchancery.org
Mobile: +254-721-222 311

For
The Centre for Christian-Muslim Relations in Eastleigh (CCMRE)
St. Paul's University
Private Bag
Limuru 00217, Kenya

ISBN 978-9966-040-61-9

To all men and women who believe in peace

Contents

Acknowledgements	*1*
Foreword by Dr. Hasan Kinyua	*2*
Foreword by Prof. Esther Mombo	*3*
Introduction: Mapping this Book *by Willem Jansen*	*5*
Chapter One: Mapping the Contexts of Eastleigh *by Willem Jansen*	*10*
Chapter Two: Mapping the Diversity of Eastleigh *by Halkano Abdi Wario*	*21*
Chapter Three: Mapping Eastleigh as a Public Platform: The World of Street Preachers *by Joseph Wandera*	*26*
Chapter Four: A Street Preacher's Da'wah*by Ibrahim Issack*	*35*
Chapter Five: A Sūfī Perspective on Christian-Muslim Relations in Eastleigh and Beyond *by Sufi Merabaqsh Abdulaziz Bunni*	*36*
Chapter Six: Mapping Eastleigh for Christian-Muslim Relations: A Project Report *by C.B. Peter*	*44*
Chapter Seven: How Mapping Can Build Christian-Muslim Relations *by Willem Jansen*	*62*
Appendix 1: The Eastleigh Mapping Pictorial by Willem Jansen and C. B. Peter	*68*
Appendix 2: List of Contributors	*85*
Appendix 3: List of Mappers	*86*
Appendix 4: Recommendation letter of Supreme Council of Kenyan Muslims (SUPKEM)	*87*

Acknowledgements

We thank Prof. Esther Mombo (DVC-AA) of St. Paul's University for her support of CCMRE, as expressed in her Foreword. We acknowledge the Supreme Council of Kenyan Muslims (SUPKEM) in the person of Dr. Hassan Kinyua for its moral support as expressed in his Foreword. Moreover, the SUPKEM recommendation letter proved to be very helpful during the project in winning the confidence of the "Eastleighans". We further want to express our gratitude to all the contributors to this volume. We acknowledge Dr. Halkano Abdi Wario for his contribution to this book and his help in getting, and keeping, the Eastleigh-mappers on board with the project throughout. We thank *sūfī* sheikh Merabaqsh Abdul-Aziz for his contribution to this book and for his enthusiastic support of the CCMRE project at large. We acknowledge the work of student Bernadette Massaquoi and her eagerness to learn through active participation, and especially her valuable help in mapping data processing and analysis. Susan Olulo and Katuma Mohammed—one of the "mapping pairs"—gave their permission to tell their rather personal story, for which we are grateful. We thank Ibrahim Issack and Salim Ndeeda, for their contribution to this book. We are especially grateful to Kirsten Krymusa for her help in matters of English language, proofreading and general advice. We thank all St. Paul's University and Eastleigh students for their dedication and patience. Without them, we would not have been able to bring the project to a success. We thank the Eastleigh Fellowship Centre (Mennonite) for hosting us and also for their active participation. Last but certainly not least, we thank *Kerk in Actie* (Church in Action) of the Protestant Church in The Netherlands for their financial and prayerful support of the CCMRE project right from the start.

Editors

Foreword

Interfaith forums help disseminate comprehensive knowledge which may help to supply basic needs, social services, counseling, and economic development by empowering the world with peace and harmony.

All the Prophets of Allah initiated Interfaith Communities in their own times whenever there were interfaith issues to address such as economics, business, and trade so as to make sure that there were no under-served people in any area. Remember the Prophet Muhammad and the first Constitution of Medina, this was an interfaith initiative to make sure that Christians and Jews live comfortably under Islamic rule.

This publication is an emulation of the Prophets' projects by creating interfaith relations making it able to collaborate to make a bigger impact on our world.

The publication provides an evolving interfaith approach which can lead into a broad continuum of programs and services that provides the tools and resources people in crisis need to stabilize and rebuild their lives.

We the Supreme Council of Kenya Muslim (SUPKEM) commend reading of this publication which will enhance Interfaith cooperation in our societies.

We also congratulate the authors, editors and also readers for their outstanding level of commitment in making sure that all faithful live in peace and harmony.

If you are searching for tools to creative governance of Interfaith issues, collaborative interfaith task forces and committees, or organize special events and fundraising for interfaith activities then this book will equip you with invaluable expertise and insight to further the mission of interfaith relations.

Enjoy the book!

Dr. Sheikh Hassan Kinyua Omari
Director-Religious Affairs
Supreme Council of Kenya Muslims (SUPKEM)

Foreword

St. Paul's University (SPU) in line with its vision and mission has been on the frontline of preparing courses that are relevant to society at large. Islam and Christian-Muslim relations, HIV and AIDS, and leadership development are some of the areas where SPU offers creative and innovative opportunities. For a number of years now the university has run a postgraduate Diploma and MA degree programme in Islam and Christian-Muslim Relations. The context of this is the fact that Christians and Muslims form the majority of Kenya. The course is aimed at providing skills and tools for positive Christian-Muslim engagement in Dialogue for peaceful co-existence. In our contemporary situation, dialogue has become indispensable as a means of preventing conflict and as a tool for conflict resolution. Religious dialogue, unlike other forms of dialogue, however, has to be done in the context which defines people's fears and aspirations. The context is not limited to religion but encompasses the social, economic and political realities of all people. The course content requires students to objectively study Islam and Christian-Muslim relations (historical and contemporary), in theory and to experience working together in a given context.

Teaching this course would not be complete unless there was a lived experience for students and faculty to engage and experience Christian-Muslim relations in a lived, local context. It is against this background that the SPU Centre for Christian-Muslim Relations in Eastleigh (CCMRE) was founded. As shown in this book, Eastleigh lately has been in the limelight for negative reasons due to incidents of insecurity allegedly masterminded by members of the *Al-Shabaab group*. The mapping exercise undertaken as a collaborative project between Muslim and Christian students is to show that a shared study and mapping of common space can indeed help foster Christian-Muslim relations. Eastleigh is a haven of activities where both Muslims and Christians struggle to survive through social, economic and political realities. The faith of the different people is reflected in the religious spaces within Eastleigh. The mapping exercise brings out the realities of the different communities in Eastleigh and helps to deal with the perceived suspicions and tensions among them.

The mapping exercise as shown in this book brings to light another way of experiencing relationships. It is not historical and theological issues alone that have divided the communities but also the issue ofcontested space. The shared space reveals the realities of struggle for both communities. The mapping exposure increases the visibility of SPU students to different realities and also invites the Muslim students to the opportunities of studying Islam and Christian-Muslim relations.

The findings and recommendations from the mapping exercise will inform the general research communities interested in understanding interfaith relations against the backdrop of spatiality. The findings will further strengthen the teaching of the course for enhancing it to meet its objectives, which include the provision of necessary tools for Christian-Muslim positive engagement, doing Christian mission in an interfaith milieu, and appreciating the Christian-Muslim presence in Eastleigh Kenya and its meaning for Christian living.

Prof. Esther Mombo
Deputy Vice Chancellor (Academic Affairs)
St. Paul's University, Limuru, Kenya

INTRODUCTION

Mapping this Book

Willem Jansen

The book in your hands is the first publication of the Centre for Christian-Muslim Relations in Eastleigh (CCMRE). This Centre was established in 2010 by St. Paul's University (SPU), in Limuru, Kenya, as one of the University's practical programmes, in the area of Christian-Muslim relations. The CCMRE was established as a result of the joint efforts of Joseph Wandera and the present writer, and is co-managed by them on behalf of St. Paul's University.

Since 2004, St. Paul's University in cooperation with churches and church-related organizations in Africa, Europe and the USA, and the Programme for Christian-Muslim Relations in Africa (PROCMURA), has been running a Master's Programme in Islam and Christian-Muslim Relations (ICMR). The ICMR-programme has attracted students, from many sub-Saharan countries such as Kenya, Tanzania, Madagascar, the Sudan, Rwanda, Nigeria, Liberia and Sierra Leone. However, the number of students has remained low due to, - amongst other reasons - the lack of a practical dimension in the largely academic approach.

While the ICMR programme upholds its mission of academic excellence, the CCMRE project seeks to supplement the theoretical study with a more practical approach of interreligious dialogue and the reflection on dia*praxis*[1], or dialogue in practice. The CCMRE, with its physical location on Eighth Street, Eastleigh, in Nairobi, Kenya, aims at enabling ICMR students to become both scholars and practitioners. By means of exposure programmes conducted at the ICMR, students and scholars have opportunities to supplement their theoretical knowledge with practical skills that can be used in their respective congregations, parishes, mosque-related organizations, and in the wider society.

The CCMRE vision is: (1) To expand the cooperation and information-exchange between adult educators and academics, belonging to different faiths, by participating in different projects in sub-Saharan Africa; and (2) To identify, test and evaluate methodological approaches and concepts of interreligious and intercultural dialogue, in order to develop these

---

[1] The term "diapraxis" denotes dialogue within an action-reflection praxis context. Thus dialogue between Christians and Muslims is not merely a verbal *mihadhara* or discursive debate. It is actually an existential participation in real life. Such an approach establishes the Eastleigh mapping exercise within the basic theoretical framework.

further by accommodating the learning needs of Christian and Muslim individuals in the Kenyan context of Eastleigh.

Beyond the individual learning processes, group-learning techniques are applied at the Centre. The CCMRE project has, therefore, formulated the following objectives:

- To achieve a better understanding of dialogue between Christians and Muslims and its necessary socio-political conditions,
- To recognize and overcome stereotypes,
- To encourage all parties (Christians, Muslims, non- and other-believers) to take part in the project,
- To demonstrate that, in spite of historical, cultural and political diversity, scholars, adult educators, students and guests of the Centre can learn from each other in the processes of the CCMRE activities; and,
- To facilitate, organise and publish academic research in the field of intercultural and interreligious studies, e.g. seminars, and workshops that are made public by academic articles, books, and audio-video materials.

During the first two years of the CCMRE project, the team has realised these objectives through academic and practical programmes, such as exposure tours in Eastleigh for students and scholars at all levels; critical evaluation of good practices in Christian-Muslim relations elsewhere in Africa; and a mapping project.

The report of the mapping project that took place between November 2012 and February 2013, has been presented by C.B. Peter in Chapter Six of this book. It is introduced and followed by five chapters and appendices, all related to the "mapped" phenomena of the intriguing estate of Eastleigh, Nairobi. The mapping project of the CCMRE, which brought together students and staff from various religious and cultural backgrounds, shows Christian-Muslim relations in *action*. That is exactly what St. Paul's University's Centre for Christian-Muslim Relations in Eastleigh (CCMRE) stands for: academic and practical programmes, that attempt to build bridges between faith communities. Muslims and Christians are actually *working* together through dia*praxis*, or dialogue in practice, rather than having interreligious discursive dialogue by words alone.

Mapping Eastleigh

"Mapping" is a rather new development within theology, taking seriously insights from postmodern geography and spatiality theories. This method of mapping, in the sense of 'observing a place in order to gain existential knowledge about it', has recently become a tool of theological reflection. St. Paul's University senior lecturer Peter's Ph.D. research specializes in this new field. Peter introduces the approach as follows:

> The celebrated postmodern theorist Michele Foucault has noted that our times are characterized by a decline of historicism. In other words, space seems to have gained prominence over time. Geography seems to have usurped the power of history. Place is no longer a passive entity to be inhabited. Maps are no longer mere navigational devices to facilitate the historical pursuits of explorers. On the contrary, space has now become an

ideological production (Henri Lefebvre). Place holds a certain power over its inhabitants and even those outside it (Literary Geography). The stark realities of rapid urbanization have created a whole new virtual universe which has sucked us into it via celluloid screens (Urban Geography)[2].

Peter has traced the theoretical nuances of "this monumental point in postmodern history", the defining moment towards space and place, which in our times has come to be known as "The Spatial Turn". Thus, according to Peter, mapping human-occupied space, more than producing merely objective, gadget-generated natural maps, can actually offer us with

> [A] catalogue of the major areas where theological implications of the spatial turn could be most visible. Creation of space is no longer the populist hat-trick of the theological magician. The monster has already emerged. It is for us theologians to decide what to do with it. Come, let us write the new *Summa Theologia* with the help of maps that we construct as a result of our phenomenological engagement with space and place![3]

Thus mapping, the context of the present book, is a study of place in relation to people. In this way, maps are communication of ideas as well. Through his Ph.D. research, Peter is investigating the role of mapping in theological reflection. As the major development in the postmodern era (since 1950), the French approach focusing on place/space has gained prominence over the English-German approach focusing on history/time. Peter points to three prominent developments in human geography: (1) large scale population displacements, (2) urban migrations, and (3) the rise of industrial cities. These three points are all relevant to Eastleigh's environs, as will be described in Chapter One.

This new approach in theology Peter coins as the 'the spatial turn in theology'. Addressing the question *"What has geography to do with theology?"*, Peter identifies four major premises where mapping would have a bearing on theological reflection: (1) Theology is a reflective project, (2) Our existential self-understanding plays a significant role in this reflection, (3) Our phenomenological engagement with place contributes to our existential self-understanding, and (4) Therefore, our map-making and map-interpretation can contribute to our theological reflection.[4]

All communities exist in places, and without place there can be no people. Since all communities need space, space often becomes contested space, especially when communities cannot relate to each other well. Here issues of justice come to the fore—matters of social justice, gender justice, political and economic justice. In the present study the question of justice in the context of Eastleigh—as an ethnic, economic and religious place—is of paramount importance. Thus in the context of Christian-Muslim relations marked by mutual suspicion, intolerance, negative ethnicity, job insecurity, real or perceived marginalisation, discrimination, and security-related issues, amongst others, mapping becomes a 'reflection-exercise'. The study of place could then be helpful in our self-understanding.

---

[2] C. B. Peter, *"The Spatial Turn and Theology."* Unpublished PowerPoint Presentation St. Paul's University Faculty Research Seminar, 25/10/2012.
[3] Peter, ibid.
[4] Ibid.

Eastleigh has previously been "mapped" for different, non-theological variables. Some of the earlier mapping projects in Eastleigh include: (1) Mapping Eastleigh for Sexual Gender Based Violence (SGBV) in 2012,[5] (2) Mapping Eastleigh for youth organisations and political, social and religious organisations in which 53 youth organizations and a few other organizations were mapped,[6] (3) the dissertation by Anna Jacobsen (2011)[7] with a "mapping" perspective, and (4) Local initiatives such as the Justice and Peace Committee of the Catholic Church St. Teresa, mapping unreported crime in Eastleigh.

The CCMRE project, in November 2012, took the initiative, for the first time, to map the twelve streets in Section I of Eastleigh for Christian-Muslim relations. Mosques, churches and affiliated organisations—called Faith Based Organisations (FBO's)—were mapped together with other community assets such as places of commercial, social and economic importance. The aims and objectives of this three days project were: (a) To publish a mapping report for Christian-Muslim relations in Eastleigh to assist further research by national and international visitors, researchers and others interested in the work of the CCMRE, (b) to foster Christian-Muslim Relations (CMR) in Eastleigh, and (c) to use the experiment as a catalyst to foster CMR in the wider context of Kenya.

The mapping method we used was guided by the following six steps: (1) Twelve SPU students and twelve students from Eastleigh (total 24) were selected and invited to the research project at the CCMRE, Eighth Street, Eastleigh. (2) The CCMRE staff introduced the project to the students and invited C.B. Peter as the specialist in the field of mapping from a theological perspective to highlight the technique, tools, practice and evaluation of mapping. (3) Between 15 and 17 November 2012, the SPU students and Muslim students from Eastleigh went in twelve 'mixed' pairs, to map the twelve streets of Eastleigh Section I by identifying, (through taking pictures; conducting interviews and collecting further data) the FBOs and other community assets found on each of the twelve streets. (4) At their return to the CCMRE, the teams used the data to construct maps. These maps were presented at a plenary meeting. The researchers were given a certificate and a small honorarium to appreciate their participation in the exercise, and, (5) On February 8th 2013, the data were jointly analysed and edited by a mixed group of scholars and students, who had participated in the project. The sixth chapter of the present publication contains all the details of this fascinating mapping project in the form of a report.

Other Chapters in this Book

The book begins with a chapter by Willem Jansen on Eastleigh's history and its socio-economic and political contexts. He focuses on the religious trends and issues that one comes across when frequenting this part of Kenya's capital city. He considers the religious discourse between representatives of Wahhābī and Sūfī shades of Islam in Eastleigh to be one of the

---

[5] Conducted by Refuge Point.
[6] Conducted by USAID.
[7] Jacobsen, A. 2011 "*Making Moral Worlds: Individual and Social Processes of Meaning-Making in a Somali Diaspora*".

most pertinent issues at stake. There are also a number of chapters describing the many faces of this intriguing suburb of Eastleigh, either from a *Sūfī*-mystic perspective (Merabaqsh Abdul-Aziz), or a *mihadhara* (public debate) perspective—from both scholarly (Joseph Wandera, who recently completed his Ph.D. on this phenomenon of *mihadhara*) as well as from populist (Ibrahim Issack and Salim Ndeeda) angles. Then we also have a chapter by Dr. Halkano Abdi Wario highlighting the contrasts of the "Eastleigh experience". Then there is the story of Susan Olulo and Kaltuma Mohammed, who happened to meet each other for the CCMRE project, and worked together as a "mixed mapping pair". That which started by finding out each other's origin and religion, gradually developed into a cautious friendship.

In the appendices one can find some supplementary resources. Under the title "Mapping Pictorial", the reader will finally be shown some photos of this project *in action*. A list of the Mappers and a list of some biographic data of the contributors to this book as a whole are included in the appendices as well.

If this book can generate some new knowledge of Eastleigh spatiality with reference to Christian-Muslim relations, it has been worth the effort. If, on the other hand, it can evoke deeper analysis and critique as to how mapping can be a useful tool in transforming people's perceptions of Christian-Muslim relations, then indeed it will be truly rewarding to all who embody this book—authors, editors, publishers, participating researchers, and above all, you—constant reader!

CHAPTER ONE

Mapping the Contexts of Eastleigh

Willem Jansen

Abstract

In this chapter the historical, demographic, socio-economic and religious context of Eastleigh, Nairobi, Kenya is described. Some facts and figures about the Estate are given, alongside some more general features. A brief historical overview of Eastleigh will help readers to understand Eastleigh's context from a primarily Somali migration perspective. The focus of this article is on the distinct religious phenomena one encounters in Eastleigh, such as utterances of Muslim faith (īmān) and culture. At the end of the article the discursive mihadhara ('public debates') are juxtaposed to the Muslim mystical, sūfī-practices, and it is argued that the latter are to be preferred over the former, in terms of genuine Christian-Muslim relations.

Introduction

Eastleigh is a Nairobi suburb sprawling with economic activity and largely populated by Somali Muslims. It is a just a few kilometres away from Nairobi's city centre. Since 2009 it has become easier to reach Eastleigh. Travelling via Limuru Road, where St. Paul's University is located, and Muthaiga road we quite easily reach our destination. Chinese road construction companies have recently finalized Super Highways, connecting Muthaiga Road and Thika Road, from which Eastleigh can now be entered directly. As soon as we enter the Estate, however, the road becomes pock-marked. Therefore, to save our car from another garage visit, whenever we frequent Eastleigh, we park our car at the entrance of Eastleigh at St. Teresa's Catholic Church.

At the church gate, some street boys, in tattered brownish clothing and broken flip-flops, do not seem to even register the still rare phenomenon of a *mzungu*[8] accompanied by his Kenyan colleague, passing by. A few hundred meters from the Catholic Church, on the 18th of November 2012, the students of St. Paul's University heard an explosion. People were screaming in the Church compound and many people where running away from the spot of the blast. We learnt that a device had been detonated in a *matatu*-bus - the local means of transport - allegedly by the *al-Qaida*-linked group of *al-Shabaab*[9]. This was yet another act of terror in a context of (inter)national political tensions. The security[10] issue continues to be a factor to be reckoned with throughout our presence and activities, in this intriguing place.

---

[8] Ki-Swahili, literally 'a person who wanders', referring to a white person or foreigner.
[9] The allegation that *Al-Shabaab* (Arabic for 'the youth') was behind the attack, has not been proven. An officer of a main mosque of Nairobi, whom I happened to encounter in his hometown of Lamu, in December 2012, suggested that Kikuyu traders and politicians might have been behind the atrocity.
[10] One of the security issues concerns the youth groups considered as criminal gangs such as "Super Power", "Silly Blue", and "*Sikujui*" (ki-Swahil, "I don't know you").

The Centre for Christian-Muslim Relations in Eastleigh (CCMRE) can hardly be reached by car, let alone parked, in the midst of the piles of garbage. So we walk, as part of our weekly exposure, from First Street to Eighth Street. Eastleigh Section I, located in the dusty and muddy east of the city, is laid out in a chessboard-like street pattern, intersected by 12 streets in east-west orientation. Somalis and non-Somalis[11] alike call this area "Little Mogadishu" because of the huge number of Somalis amongst the approximately 200,000 inhabitants[12]. There are mosques, churches and affiliated Faith Based Organisations (FBO's) in almost every building. Street preachers dot the Estate, especially the lively markets. The numerous shops, shopping-malls and kiosks, decorated with Islamic religious expressions and names, are primarily owned and operated by Somalis.

A Short History of Eastleigh

Nairobi was founded in 1896 as a station of the 'East African Railway', half way between Mombasa on the Indian Ocean and Kisumu on Lake Victoria. South-Asians, most of them having Indian background, started settling in the city. At that time hardly any local Kenyan population was living in Nairobi. Kenyans were only allowed to live within the boundary of the city as bachelors and if they had formal employment by one of the white settlers, or by one of the companies in the young city. Their families had to reside in villages beyond the city limits or in other parts of the country. Indian and Arabic traders who had dominated trade along the east African coast played an essential part in the construction of the train line (Herz M., 2010). The colonial government put residence zones in place, based on racial segregation. Together with the neighbouring estates of Pangani and Ngara, the Eastleigh part of Nairobi was allocated to the South-Asians as the area of residence and trade[13].

What is now the eastern Nairobi suburb of Eastleigh was open savannah where wild animals roamed before Asians, Arabs, Somalis, and other Africans were pushed into it by the European settlers (Micheni M., 2010: 26). Thus, Eastleigh was officially established as a human settlement by the colonial government in 1912 for Asians and some wealthy Africans (Jacobsen A., 2011: 71). The first groups of Somalis came to Nairobi as escorts and guards for British Empire builders. A few others came to work on the Kenya-Uganda railway. Under the protection of the colonial power, Somalis started their businesses alongside the Asians and Europeans in Nairobi, before they had to move around 1920 to this bushy place, which by then was called *Kampi ya Somali* (Ki-Swahili for 'Somali camp')[14].

It was not until the 1930s that *Kampi ya Somali* changed its name to Eastleigh. After the Royal Air Force had built what is presently Moi Military Airport, just behind Twelfth Street, most of the troops that were sent there came from Eastleigh in Hampshire in the UK. These soldiers probably attempted to make themselves 'at home' by renaming the place. Till this

---

[11] Kenyans, for instance, call the area 'Mogadisho Kidogo' (Ki-Swalihi, 'Little Mogadisho'). Many Kenyans consider the place not to be part of Kenya, though geographically/physically it, of course, is. (Cf. Jacobsen, 2011: 83, note 47).

[12] The number of residents of Eastleigh varies from roughly 100,000 (*Refuge Point* 2011) to over 300,000 (*Daily Nation*, September 26th 2010), depending on the neighbourhoods that are counted as part of the Estate. The issue of refugees without legal status, and passers-by business people, make it hard to give exact figures.

[13] For this information I am indebted to scholar Halkano Abdi Wario, who is one of the contributors to this book.

[14] "The racial categories of the British Colonialists placed the Somalis in ambiguous positions. There were three main divisions: Whites (top), Asians which included Arabs (sandwich/middle) and Africans (bottom). The Somalis were classified as Asians [...] and also insisted on preferential treatments and rights to settle in towns in certain instances" (personal comment of Halkano Abdi Wario).

day the Kenyan Defence Force (KDF) are encamped in the area. In October 2011, when the KDF entered Somalia for a military mission, I was told that the Barakat-hotel[15] and other high buildings near the Airport were under scrutiny because of possible rocket attacks from their roofs.

During the 1940s a law was passed which allowed the left-behind Kenyan families to join their men, husbands and fathers in Nairobi. This coincided with the growing wealth of the trading community, enabling especially the Indians to move to the better neighbourhoods of Westlands and Parklands towards the west of the city. Nairobi's east, and especially Eastleigh, was thus again to become an "immigrant's" neighbourhood, this time for a population of local Kenyans, all moving into the colonial capital for the first time. With the political independence of Kenya in 1963, segregation of residential spaces along ethnic lines was abolished and the population of Nairobi increased considerably. Along with the Kenyans from villages and rural areas, some Somali traders had moved to Eastleigh and settled there.

Meanwhile, the Somali President Siad Barre was overthrown in 1991. Civil war broke out in the country in the Horn of Africa[16]. Somalia disintegrated more and more, suffering from famine, lack of basic needs and the destruction of its infrastructure, and slid into the condition of a failed state. Within a short time hundreds of thousands of Somalis fled over the border into Kenya. They were placed into refugee camps near the Kenyan city of Dadaab, and were reduced to a dismal existence in this disconnected part of the country. A famine in 2011 in the Dadaab camp and its environs triggered world-wide attention.

The Kenyan government, which had previously practiced liberal and generous refugee policies and had granted refugees full mobility within the whole country, now opted for a much more restricted system, facing the large increase in the refugee flow. From now on, all refugees had to reside in the camps and were not allowed to take up work. The refugee camps in the east of the country, disconnected due to bad infrastructural connections, become virtual open air prisons. International human rights organizations, such as Amnesty International, have criticized the Kenyan government for neglecting these refugees under international law standards[17].

A considerable percentage of the people who flee from Somalia are previously well-to-do traders, mostly from the capital of Mogadishu. They have come from an urban background and are not used to the rural way of life in the refugee camps. Having sold off their goods and real estate shortly before their escape to Kenya, they arrive in Nairobi with their wealth. As they are used to an urban way of life and with the lack of possibilities of trade in the refugee camps, they move towards Nairobi's city centre. Supported by the pre-existing contacts with the Somalis that have lived in Kenya's capital for a longer time, they often move to Eastleigh.

---

[15] This high-end, new hotel, was built by and for Somalis now living in Europe and North America. In the hotel the Transitional Federal Government used to hold meetings, before the new government was put in place in October 2012.

[16] To understand the root causes of the civil war, some have identified "contemporary politicized clan identities", while others trace the cause back to "colonial governments essentialised clan identities" and "capital economy and the rise of the middle class over and against the desires of the largely nomadic population" (Jacobsen, 2011: 61).

[17] *"Kenya's Somali refugee plan unlawful, says Amnesty"* BBC Online, 21st December 2012: www.bbc.co.uk/news/world-africa-20819462 (accessed 14 April 2013).

However, there are also very deprived Somali migrants who arrive with no money or immigration papers in search of security and a better life in Eastleigh and perhaps beyond. Such are the contrasts that one finds in Eastleigh today. Thus, for its third time[18], Eastleigh has become an immigrant's quarter, this time for wealthy Somali refugees who are rehabilitating themselves and using Eastleigh as a market place, both with official identity papers and without.

Demography of Eastleigh

As alluded to earlier in this study, Kenya is considered a relatively stable entity in the East Africa region. Kenya has, however, experienced a rapid and large-scale influx of refugees fleeing crises and insecurity in neighbouring countries throughout the past 20 years. The number of current registered refugees residing in Kenya has grown from approximately 12,000 in 1988 to over 616,000 in 2012, with 93 percent of those current registered residents originating from the Horn of Africa.

While it has never been an official Kenyan policy, since the early 1990s the country has in practice required refugees to reside in camps. There are currently four camps in Kenya, three located around Dadaab, near the Somali border in north-eastern Kenya, and one in Kakuma in the north-west. Together, these camps are home to 88% of Kenya's refugees. There are, however, a number of administrative exceptions to the 'encampment policy'.

As of May 2012, the official number of registered asylum seekers and refugees in Nairobi (and therefore not in camps) was over 54,000, but unofficial estimates posit that there could be as many as 100,000. Despite the large numbers, urban refugees remain a 'hidden' and neglected population that has been 'absorbed into the urban fabric; they are dispersed over the city and remain highly mobile'. According to UNHCR, there are over 20,000 registered refugees and asylum-seekers of Somali origin in Nairobi, the great majority in Eastleigh district. This figure does not include many thousands of unregistered refugees. Some estimates put the number of Somali refugees in Eastleigh alone at 60,000. Ethiopians are the second largest nationality in Eastleigh.

According to UNHCR, over 12,000 refugees and asylum seekers of Ethiopian origin have taken up residence in Nairobi. They belong to various ethnic groups, primarily Oromos and Amhara, and a small number of Anuak. The great majority of Oromos and Amhara live in Eastleigh. Eastleigh has also attracted refugees from Eritrea and Sudan, and other countries in the Horn of Africa such as Djibouti and Central and Southern Africa. Somalis and Ethiopians tend to concentrate in Eastleigh, while South-Sudanese may be found scattered in several locations, including Eastleigh.

Socio-economic and Political Context of Eastleigh

Initially, Somali traders come to Nairobi with the aim of settling administrative affairs, such as identity papers, in order to quickly move on to London, Dubai or the United States. Hotels, guesthouses and other kinds of lodgings have been constructed where they can pass the time waiting to receive their exit visas. One of these guesthouses 'Garissa Lodge', is located on 1st Avenue and named after a Kenyan town in the east of the country inhabited by ethnic

---

[18] Sufi Sheikh Merabaqsh Abdulaziz, whom I came to know at the CCMRE, has lived his entire life in Eastleigh. He described the different groups of these three 'waves' of immigrants as: (1) during his early child hood, the Whites, the Hindus and the Somali 'tycoons'; (2) the Kenyans, before and after independence in 1963, and (3) the huge influx of Somalis since the 70s and 80s.

Somalis[19]. The refugees come with considerable amounts of money to Nairobi and often have to linger for months before finishing their immigration documents, amongst others. They start spending their time doing business and trading goods. As they cannot, or do not want to, set up their own infrastructure of trading spaces, they start doing business from their hotel rooms. Garissa Lodge has thus slowly transformed itself from an accommodation space to a trading place.

Garissa Lodge was eventually transformed into a shopping mall. This Somali trading centre in Eastleigh was quickly replicated with many variations constructed along Eastleigh's main road. Trading acts as an attractor, and the number of Somali refugees in Eastleigh rose quickly with today, as already mentioned above, an estimated 200,000 people living in the streets of "Little Mogadishu".

Eastleigh has become one of the biggest business hubs in East Africa, if not the biggest. Hundreds of trading women[20] and men compete for customers from all corners of the country and the countries surrounding Kenya. In the main Section 1 there are 30 shopping malls, 6,000 shops, and 11 banks. Of the residential houses, 95% are commercial and only 5% private[21]. Eastleigh seems to be well-networked with the rest of the business world. Informal services called *hawala* facilitate the rapid cash-transfer to the Somali Diaspora throughout the world[22].

Besides this international network for business, Eastleigh has allegedly also become one of the most important links with Somali-based militants and the outside world: "Businessmen, foreign donors, fundraisers and other sources supporting the insurgents channel funds into this sprawling neighbourhood through the discreetly effective hawala"[23]. Analysts also say that the area is being used as a money laundering base. This closed economic system seems to frustrate some Kenyans that I spoke to, saying that ordinary Kenyans cannot compete with the Somali in paying the rent, or even buying houses in Eastleigh. Pavanello (2010: 24) describes this rather awkward situation as follows:

> Many landlords in Eastleigh are happy to rent accommodation without a regular contract, as long as three months' rent is paid in advance. Refugees who do not have legal documents often ask other refugees to sign the tenancy agreement on their behalf. This usually generates a mark-up on rent as refugees with no legal documents will usually be asked to pay a higher price than agreed on the tenancy agreement. This seems to have become a lucrative business, especially among Somali refugee communities in Eastleigh. Somali refugees with legal papers often rent accommodation from Kenyan landlords and then sub-let it to paperless refugees. Kenyan landlords, often of Kikuyu origin, are aware of these transactions but do not question

---

[19] Ethnicity as such is generally seen as having positive and negative shades and meanings. In Kenya the Somalis are seen as the 42nd "tribe". According to the Kenyan census of 2009, with its 2,4 million, - from which officially 400.000 are refugees - the Somalis are the sixth by size (*Kenyan Census,* August 2009). The Somalis themselves are divided into 6 "clan families", i.e.; Darood, Hawiye, Isaaq, Dir, Digil and Rahanweyn. Hawiye, the main group in Eastleigh come originally from in and around Mogadishu (Griffiths 2002: 32).

[20] Through her Ph.D.-research in Eastleigh, Jacobsen discovered Somali women being the "back-bone'" of Somali society. In Eastleigh, every woman she talked to "lived in a female-headed household, in which not only was the woman the primary breadwinner, but she was also responsible... for the allocation for resources to various tasks and purchases" (Jacobsen, A. 2011: 31).

[21] Eastleigh Business District Association, in: *Daily Sunday*, 26th September 2010: 27.

[22] One of my contacts, Mr. Abdisalat from the CCMRE's neighbouring Eighth Street mosque, explained to me how, within minutes, he could withdraw money from his bank account in Eastleigh after an international phone call with his daughter in The Netherlands.

[23] Samora M. In: *Daily Sunday*, 26th September 2010: 27.

the sub-letting as they prefer to deal with reliable intermediaries. Somali sub-letters also prefer to deal with Somali middlemen rather than Kenyan landlords directly.

This renting situation exemplifies the plight of many Somali and of other mainly poor, urban refugees from within Kenya. During several meetings in 2010 and 2011, I met with especially Oromo and Somali women groups in Eastleigh. The women expressed their distress about their vulnerable situation. Refugees without official papers felt themselves harassed by the Kenyan police on a daily basis. Bribery, according to them, was a common way of surviving in Eastleigh. Since many of the schools, religious centres and mosques are privately owned or managed by Somalis, these all are safe havens, where the women felt relative autonomy and where they could leave Kenyan police behind (Cf. Jacobsen, 2011: 84).

The plight of Somali refugees in Eastleigh is probably best indicated by the mud and the filth. This cocktail of sewage, garbage, and dirt is ubiquitous in all the streets. Outbreaks of cholera and dysentery are always lurking. Homeless individuals and drug addicts live amidst this garbage and filth. Some large trash piles are said to be used as a "dumpsite for abandoned newborns and aborted foetuses" (Jacobsen 2011: 80). All in all, Eastleigh has become a place where basic human dignity seems to be at stake[24].

The Kenyan government seems to show little attention and appears generally apathetic towards the plight of Eastleigh's residents. The minimal infrastructure provided by the authorities[25], leaves the place not only strewn with dirt and garbage almost everywhere, but also as a socially, politically and criminally unpredictable place. As mentioned above, large scale sexual gender-based violence has been mapped in the area. The Kenyan security officers in the area have recently become involved in fighting the terrorist group of *al-shabaab* that has become active, especially after the alleged defeat of the group in Kismayu, Somalia, in October 2012. Also, the war and livestock theft that characterizes the relationship between clans in Somalia and the North-Western provinces of Kenya represents an inter-clan hostility, frequently of long standing[26]. In many cases the Kenyan security forces can only react to the terrorist activities. On December 7th 2012, even the Somali MP Yusuf Hassan[27] was attacked in Eastleigh, but survived the blast (*Daily Nation*, 8th December 2012).

---

[24] And yet I have noticed the big divide between the awkward infrastructural outer appearance of Eastleigh and the cleanliness of the buildings, shopping malls, offices banks and residential houses. This is why Jacobsen could map Eastleigh as "a quintessential moral and therefore clean place" (2011: 75), even "a moral Mecca in an immoral Nairobi" (2011:86) of the Somali Diaspora.

[25] Interestingly, the electricity supply to business hub Eastleigh by the same governmental companies is well catered for, as we learnt from the mapping exercise. Probably this is because of huge income generated by providing electricity, whereas building decent roads and other infrastructural services such as sewage and drinking water systems, are allegedly not worth the investment of the local authorities.

[26] In November 2012, 39 police officers were ambushed and killed in such a case in Samburu District.

[27] Eastleigh falls under the Nairobi county of Kamukunji constituency and has a number of county wards. Yusuf Hassan, the current MP, is a Somali Kenyan" (personal comment Halkano Abdi Wario). The personal adviser of Mr. Hassan, Sheikh Abdul Nasser, I found in distress, answering my phone call from the ward of Aga Khan Hospital. Two weeks before the event, Sheikh Nasser had introduced me to Mr. Hassan, who then spontaneously promised to visit the CCMRE. This attack on Yusuf Hassan was hardly featured in the media, both in Kenya and abroad. When some months before this event, however, churches in Nairobi and Garissa were attacked, this was covered on front pages in the national and international media.

Islamic Religious Context of Eastleigh

In line with nineteenth century anthropologist Tylor, Ellis and Ter Haar have developed a working definition of religion in the present context of Africa: "Religion in sub-Saharan Africa is best considered as a belief in the existence of an invisible world, distinct but not separate from the visible one, that is home to spiritual beings with effective powers over the material world" (Ellis and Ter Haar 2007:387). In the economic hot spot of Eastleigh, these material and religious worlds seem indeed to go hand in hand.

In Eastleigh, the relationship people have with the spirit world represents an everyday reality that constitutes how they experience life and how they practice faith and morality. Spirit possession in the context of Eastleigh involves communication and interaction with spirits who maintain the moral order (Lewis, 1991 in: Jacobsen 2011: 129). Amidst socio-economic and political distress, the people of Eastleigh seem to find a constant solace in their religious practice. Given their daily insecurity (financially, psychologically, socially, and other), the disciplinary practices of Islam seem to help in what the Egyptian anthropologist Saba Mahmood has called "the performance of ethical selfhood".

In the context of the present book, emphasis is laid on this practical, ethical side of religion in Eastleigh. Devotional ethical practices are considered to be the criteria for whether one is able to keep her or his faith, or īmān[28]. Imān in the context of Eastleigh, as described by anthropologist Jacobsen, is a "sort of well or reservoir often imagined as residing in a person's body, which requires constant attention" (Jacobsen, 2011: 103) Through action and activity one shows one's piety and moral self-expression, rather than by mere discourse. For instance, when a sick person sees a sheikh for treatment, it is by itself a faith-building act.

A reservoir of īmān, filled by piety-through-practice, will protect the believer from an evil *jinn*, *qarīn*, or spirit. All the devotional Islamic practices (*ibadāt*) such as prayer (*salāt*), charity (obligatory *zakāt*, and voluntary *sadaqāt*), and for many Kenyans of Somali descent, even the mystic or *sūfī* devotional act of *dhikr*, are believed to be ethical work in social relations (*mu'amalāt*). The *sūfī* quest is to experience God through moral practicalities. That is the function of *dhikr*, the remembrance of God by the recitation of his 99 names represented by the 99 beads of the Islamic equivalent of the rosary, *tasbīh*.

Sheikh Merabaksh Abdulaziz, the *sūfī*[29] by whom we were introduced to this mystical shade of Islam in Eastleigh, always wears these beads around his neck, while others sit or walk with them. He introduced us to several *dhikr* events in early 2013 in Eastleigh, at the occasion of the Maulīdi festival, celebrating the month of the Prophet's birth, in 'the Year of the Elephant' (570 CE). What we learnt from attending the *sūfīdhikrs* is especially the spiritual zeal that impacted all the participants. The youngsters of Eastleigh were given opportunity to recite, sing and meditate about their religion. We experienced hospitality by many different scents of perfume and incense. The music by the *dhov* (a drum like tambourine) was intriguing, in combination with the many different meditative movements and gestures of those present. We could never leave the site – back to the mixed odours of the dirt road - without having a meal, again with lovely smells and tastes.

---

[28] The Arabic word īmān (faith, belief) is not to be confused with *imām* (leader in prayer).
[29] The Sufis are the mystics of Islam. Their spiritual journey is to experience Allah/God. The movement has roots in early Islamic history. It first developed in Baghdad two centuries after Muhammad's *hijra* (622 AD or 0 AH) from Mecca to Medina.

Distinct *sūfī* rituals invoking the senses – rhythmic music and meditative songs, scents of perfume and incense, beautiful coloured banners, tasteful meals – we experienced to be in shrill contrast with the odours and smell that fill the streets of Eastleigh. The huge discrepancy between the cleanliness and well-organized spiritual gathering inside, and the disorganized, smelly street, is perhaps one of the most striking phenomena of the estate called Eastleigh.

The mystical tradition of Sufism, (*tassawūf*) has always been part and parcel of Somali predominantly Sunni[30] Islamic religious, cultural and even political structure. Ioan M. Lewis, a British social anthropologist and specialist of Somali religion and culture, describes how *sūfī* sheikhs with the divine grace or blessing (*baraka*) were, and still are, associated with this social, political and religious structure. These *sūfī* sheikhs have a personal chain of genealogies (*isnād*), which can be traced back to the lineage (*silsila*) of the Prophet Muhammad's clan of Quraysh. Therefore, "Somalis consider themselves as children of the Prophet" (Lewis I.M. 1998: 7).

These *sūfī* connections, according to Lewis (1998: 2), find close parallels in the social, political and religious significance of Somali clan genealogies. By these connections, Somalis can claim their direct descent from the Prophet. In this way, veneration of *sūfī* sheikhs and saints fits into the overall practice of Islam at the local, social, political and religious levels. The religious aspects of Somali genealogies, which in the pre-Islamic state of Somali society centres on sacrifice at the tombs of ancestors, throw light on the close resemblances in the religious and political functions to Somali clan genealogies. The lineage (*silsila*) of the Prophet Muhammad provided the sheikhs with their socio-political status in society.

Of all the distinct *sūfī* orders or brotherhoods (*tarīqa*, pl. *turūq*) in Somalia, in Eastleigh the Qadiriyya *tarīqa* is the most predominant one. The *dhikrs* we attended in early 2013 were organized by this Qadiriyya brotherhood. In Eastleigh, most Somalis refer to Sufis as people who practice such devotional practices as *dhikr*, as if they are a separate, autonomous group of Muslims. However, when we asked our hosts at the *dhikrs*, most *sūfī*-Muslims refer to themselves as Sunni-Muslims. When I asked the *imām* of the mosque in Tenth Street, which is known for its *sūfī* affiliation, about these distinctions within the Muslim community in Eastleigh, he seemed to get irritated, saying that there is only one Islam. Yet I discovered that over the years the internal Muslim divide has become more obvious. In the contemporary Somali context of "Little Mogadishu", the *sūfī* tradition that is so predominant in the country of origin, seems presently to be under debate.

From the early history of Islam onwards, the *sūfī* movement has had a difficult relationship with Islamic orthodoxy. At the beginning of the movement al Hallāj, a Sufi saint, was executed by impalement in 922 AD for claiming the possibility of becoming the incarnation of divine presence by saying *anā al-haq*, "I am the truth", referring to one of God's 99 attributes. David Shenk in a yet unpublished paper has observed that

> The same tensions infected Somalia when in 1909 at Biyolay a Sufi Saint, Sheikh Uways, was martyred with 26 of his disciples. The Sufi tension with orthodoxy is rooted within a paradox within the Qur'an between an insistence that there can be no fellowship between God and

---

[30] Sūnnī Islam constitutes approximately 85 percent of the Muslim population worldwide, whereas Shī'a Islam and other smaller sects constitute about 15 percent of it. Sūfism is generally not considered one of these separate sects of Islam, but is often referred to as "parallel" Islam.

humankind (*tanzih*) (Qur'an: Ikhlas: 112) and the doctrine of friendship with God (*awilya*) (Qur'an: al-Maida: 5:53-54; Jonah: 10:63).

> Sufism is not a side show within Somali Islam. All Somalis were in some way formed by Sufi spirituality. I learned that the repeated references to Allah in conversation are rooted in the Sufi commitment to remembering God as commanded in the Qur'an. "Ye who believe! Let not your riches divert you from the remembrance of God. If any act thus, the loss is their own" (Qur'an: Munafiqun: 43:9). This means that every area of life should be permeated with the remembrance of God!...Sufi piety permeates not only Somali Islam, but much of African Islam as well (D. Shenk, unpublished paper, Accra, 2010).

Thus, "perhaps the most fundamental tension in the past and today, in Somali Islam, is that between mystical mediated views of man's relation to the Prophet and to God, and more ritualistic interpretations which deny the efficacy and propriety of such human mediation with the divine" (Lewis I.M., 1998: xiii)".

Probably one of the most striking and visible discourses that are taking place among the residents of Eastleigh is that of the influence of the revivalist ideology of Wahhabism[31]. In Eastleigh this Wahhābi movement is regularly referred to as Aqwāni. This is possibly an abbreviation of *ikhwānal-muslimūn*[32], The Muslim Brotherhood that is presently in power in Egypt. What both these movements have in common is their revivalist, and even Islamist, interpretations of Islamic law, theology and socio-economic politics, and their reluctance to acknowledge Sufism (*tasawwūf*) as part of 'pure' Islam. Some *sūfī* practices such as exorcism of *jinn* and veneration of saints, are even considered 'polytheistic' (*shirk*) implying that one directs her/his entreaties at a spiritual being other than God[33].

Open-Air Preaching

Alongside the more mystical shade of Islam, another religious phenomenon that draws attention in Eastleigh is the *mihadhara*[34] (public debates). These open-air gatherings are common events throughout the Estate. *Mihadhara* can be considered one of "the Islamic methods of outreach (*da'wah*)" (John Chesworth in: Mutei J.M. 2012: x). "*Mihadhara* come in the contexts where other religions, in our case Christianity, are dominant. *Mihadhara* come up to counter the aggressive Christian outreach methods like the infamous 'crusade' method" (Mutei 2012: 74). Laurenti Magesa and Johnson Mbillah (2004) define *mihadhara* in a

---

[31] 'Wahhabism' is derived from its founder Muhammad ibn 'Abd al-Wahhab (1703-92). Hanbalism, named after Ibn Hanbal (780-855), the orthodox theologian and legal scholar, was passed on via Ibn Taymiyya (1326-1328) to Ábd al-Wahhab. Through his close relationship with the kingdom of Sa'ud, Saudi Arabia had become a Wahhabite state. The Wahhābi school of theology depended on Ibn Taymiyya's vehemence in his antagonism toward the cult of the saints in sūfī circles, and its general insistence on a return to original or purist Islam.

[32] The Muslim Brotherhood, (*jama'at al-ikhwān al-Muslimūn*) was founded in 1928 by Hassan al-Banna in Egypt, with the aim of revitalising Islam, and the re-Islamisation of people of all classes, with the ultimate aim of establishing an Islamic State, based on Islamic Law (*sharī'ah*).

[33] In Public preaching (*mihadhara*) in Eastleigh, the Christian doctrine of Trinity, falls under the category of *shirk*, which literally refers to associating, or giving partners to something/someone. In Eastleigh, the concept could also refer to 'syncretism' (Lewis 1998: 1).

[34] *Mihadhara* is the plural of the Ki-Swahili word, *Mhadhara*, probably related to an Arabic verb with the root letters *hā-da-ra*, meaning "to be present" or "to present a lecture". The Ki-Swahili verb, *kuhudhuria*, meaning "to attend", and the noun *mahudhurio*, "attendance", are derived from this Arabic verb. "Mhadhara has gained a wider, popular usage for public meetings; this includes meetings for community, political and religious purposes. Any meeting which involves the general public can be called Mhadhara" (Chesworth J. in: Mutei J.M. 2012: 30).

critical way as "public lectures by Muslim scholars, addressing issues to do with Christianity" in East-Africa, but for which "vicious polemics might seem a more adequate description".

As staff of the CCMRE we have attended several of these debates during the years that we have frequented Eastleigh. Although we might doubt whether *mihadhara* are an effective tool for interreligious discursive dialogue, preachers that present themselves briefly in this book, such as Ibrahim Issack and Salim Ndeeda, have provided us with the possibility of experiencing many welcoming and hospitable encounters with themselves and many more Muslim residents of Eastleigh. Although we acknowledge our respectful relationship with a number of the *mihadhara* participants, we do not champion the rather provocative method used during the *mihadhara* for sustainable Muslim-Christian relations.

Conclusion

In this article the historic, socio-economic, political, and religious contexts of Nairobi's Estate of Eastleigh have been outlined. For the objectives of the Centre for Christian-Muslim relations in Eastleigh (CCMRE) this community provides a rather ideal spot for experiencing and exercising durable Christian-Muslim relations. Although not altogether safe, due to all kinds of (geo) political, social and economic factors, Eastleigh still seems to be the place to be for mapping moral, cultural, and religious worlds. In religion, for instance, intra-religious trends and issues in the discussion about the place of Islam in the daily lives of the believers seem to be at high stakes. Recently, both Islamist-revivalist and *sūfī*-mystical dimensions of Islam seem to compete for the souls of Eastleigh's residents.

At the same time, however, this increased intra-religious polarisation can stimulate the more moderate inter-religious Muslim and Christian voices of Eastleigh to join hands in societal action, or *diapraxis*. Whereas the open-air public gatherings of the *mihadhara* seem to offer some self-esteem to Eastleigh's Muslim residents, at the occasions of *sūfī*-ritual practices, religious experience could possibly add more to this *diapraxis,* and therefore to the dignity of the people of Eastleigh – young and old, men and women, Muslims and non-Muslims in a context that often seems to be godforsaken.

Bibliography

Ellis S. and Ter Haar G. 2007. "Religion and Politics, taking African epistemologies seriously," *Journal of Modern African Studies* 45, 3: 383-401 pp).

Griffiths D. 2002. *Somali and Kurdish Refugees in London: New Identities in the Diaspora.* Burlington: Ashgate.

Herz M. 2010. *Somali Refugees in Eastleigh, Nairobi* (www.unhcr.org/4bOba120g.pdf).

Jacobsen, A. 2011. "Making Moral Worlds: Individual and Social Processes of Meaning-Making in a Somali Diaspora". Electronic Thesis and Dissertations. Paper 592. Saint Louis:Washington University.

Kapteijns L. 1994. *Women and the Crisis of Community Identity: The Cultural Construction of Gender in Somali History: From Catastrophe to Renewal.* Boulder: Lynne Reiner Publishers.

Lewis I.M. 1998. *Saints and Somalis, Popular Islam in a Clan-Based Society.* Lawrenceville: Red Sea Press.

Magesa L. 2005. "Contemporary Catholic Perspectives on Christian-Muslim Relations in Sub-Saharan Africa: The case of Tanzania," *Islam and Christian-Muslim Relations* 18, 2.

Mbillah J. 2004. "Interfaith Relations and the Quest for Peace in Africa", in C. Hock (ed.), *The Interface between Research and Dialogue: Christian-Muslim relations in Africa*, Münster: Litt Verlag.

Micheni M. "The making of a Somali capital base at the heart of Nairobi" *Sunday Nation*, September 26th, 2010.

Mutei J.M. 2012. *Mihadhara As a Method of Islamic Da'wah in Kenya, An Analysis of Inter-religious Dialogue in a Proselytising Context*. Nairobi: Fairfax Multimedia.

Pavanello S., Elhawary S. And Pantuliano S. 2010. *Hidden and Exposed, Urban Refugees in Nairobi, Kenya, HPG Working Paper* London: Oversees Development Institute.

CHAPTER TWO

Mapping the Diversity of Eastleigh

Halkano Abdi Wario

Abstract
This chapter seeks to describe the contrasts in Eastleigh spatiality from the dual perspectives of the author (a resident researcher in Eastleigh) and the media. The cognition of Eastleigh spatiality oscillates between the contrasting extremes of the resident's personal and subjective experience of the place on the one hand, and the media's "objective" and stereotype depiction of Eastleigh on the other; sincere religious piety on the one hand, and perpetual fear of terrorist attacks by religious fanatics on the other; dazzling affluence on the one hand, and abject poverty on the other.

Introduction

Mapping Eastleigh is an exercise in coming to grips with the contrasting diversity of this Nairobi suburb. Few places elicit such varied responses from residents and non-residents about its nature as does Eastleigh. Its fluid perception as a place of commerce competes vigorously with its long-held image as a home of diverse migrant communities from neighbouring countries and its rising enigmatic character as an insecure and precarious location. In this short reflective article, I piece together an often-overlooked cognitive view of Eastleigh as a place of many meanings, chief among them its position as an avenue for the flow of news and information from within and without, from the perspective of a resident who has conducted long term academic research in the area.

For a fascinating public display of devotional practices visit any street in Eastleigh on Fridays around 1 pm. Everything comes to a standstill when, in any of the many mosques, the call to stand for prayer is announced. The road literally turns into an extension of mosques as believers rush to form lines in readiness for prayer. Shops close, restaurants are deserted, cars stop and hushed silence descends. The only brisk businesses are those related to the sacralization of the roads: small polythene sheets are bought and sold to act as prayer-mats, making places of worship out of the busy roads.[35] Those non-Eastleigh residents caught in vehicles in the traffic of believers in devotional acts wait patiently for 10-15 minutes as

---

[35] See E. Obadare and W. Adebanwi (2010) on how would-be migrants as 'de-localized subjects' instrumentalise religion through heightened spiritual practices and symbols especially against the backdrop of the disorderly retreat of the state from the lives of ordinary people. See also P. Mandaville (2001: 116-117) who notes that many Muslims in diasporic and other forms of demographic displacements find their religion having a new symbolic significance as they transit from majority to minority status, expressed often in heightened awareness of Islam. The religion comes to play both marker of identity ('as Islam becomes a memory-aid, something with which to remember who one is') and binding factor of all followers into a transnational community of believers.

believers finish their prayers. A few minutes later it is business as usual as the congregants disperse and the roads are clear. The question that begs an answer concerns the very nature of Eastleigh, its meaning and the mental and religious attachments that the locals and visitors ascribe to it.[36]

Navigating a Neighbourhood

A simple Google search with the words 'Eastleigh Nairobi' elicits about 877,000 results. Prominent among these are news articles about the security scare and grenade attacks in the wake of heightened tensions since October 2011, following the incursion of the Kenya Defence Forces to restore order in Somalia, a neighbouring state that has been lawless since 1991. The attacks undoubtedly have earned the suburb east of Nairobi's central business district the aura of danger and uncertainty. To say you are going to Eastleigh evokes disbelief and shock from non-residents, and to claim to live there is indeed seen as a daredevil venture. Before this negative focus, a theme we shall return to later, Eastleigh enjoyed the undisputed status of vibrant business empire largely run by Somali traders, hence branded "Little Mogadishu". Its new and sparkling shopping malls share space with old buildings amidst minarets and *madrasa*s (Islamic schools), affirming the multiple meanings and purposes this neighbourhood plays that range from places of trade to sacred spaces for regular devotion and classes for religious and secular learning.

The general spatial understanding of this historical place is limited to areas around the nexus of commerce referred to as Garissa Lodge, in particular, and the twelve streets that run between and through Eastleigh First and Second Avenues in general. To come to Eastleigh is, to many non-residents, to come to Garissa Lodge for shopping and trade. The general division of Eastleigh is into three sections: Section I, the area around Juja Road; Section II, the middle section that encompasses the business centres, the twelve streets and the surrounding estates; and Section III, the residential region past the Moi Airbase located south of Eastleigh. Cognitive mapping allows the locals to distinguish the residential from commercial phases of Eastleigh, with fitting names of *Eastleigh ya Chini* (Lower Eastleigh) and *Eastleigh ya Juu* (Upper Eastleigh) respectively. The mobility between the Lower and Upper Eastleighs in the world of the Eastleighans is intense for a variety of reasons despite the ongoing infrastructural constructions.

The residents and traders in Eastleigh are from diverse backgrounds. Prominent among them are Somalis from both Kenya and Somalia, Ethiopian migrants, and other Cushitic speakers from northern Kenya. However, the rise of Eastleigh cannot be viewed in terms of diasporic demographic shifts due to the state collapse of neighbouring countries only. As mentioned in other chapters here, its emergence has its root in colonial labour migration and post-colonial rural-urban migration in search of economic opportunities and livelihood.[37] Eastleigh serves as a place of arrival and departure for many travelers to northern Kenyan towns such as Mandera, Wajir, Isiolo, Marsabit, Garissa, Moyale, Dadaab, and Kakuma, among others. As a place of first arrival, refugees from neighbouring countries find clan and filial networks to help adjust to the harsh urban conditions and needs, creating a home away from home. As a

---

[36]This reflective article is based on ethnographic research done in Eastleigh for a doctoral project between 2009 and 2012 and a lived experience as a resident of this area in the recent past.
[37]On insightful histories of Nairobi in Colonial Kenya, see Luise White (1990) *The Comfort of Home: Prostitution in Colonial Kenya* and G. R Murunga's (2005) 'Inherently Unhygienic Races": Plague and the Origins of Settler Dominance in Nairobi, 1899–1907' in *African Urban Spaces in Historical Perspective*.

place of circulation of information, it connects and networks other urban dwellers in need of news from home and who wish to properly send off their kin. For the northerners, hence, Eastleigh is an extension of an imagined 'motherland,' far and yet so near (see Anderson 1991).[38] So connected is the area to the greater Horn of Africa, one could be forgiven to think s/he is in an urban district of Mogadishu or Hargheisa, due to the diverse dialects and languages, dress and even names of business premises. The booming businesses, that range from electronic shops, casinos, bars, banks, clothing and jewelry stores, restaurants, *miraa* (*Catha edulis*, a leafy stimulant popularly consumed in Kenya) kiosks, pharmacies and clinics, schools and colleges, give Eastleigh a distinctively busy commercial status within Nairobi.

For the diverse residents, Eastleigh may be a sojourn in transit to 'greener pastures' in the West, an enterprising locale for business opportunities, a home, a place of entertainment and socialization, a shopping bazaar to buy goods or even a sacred space for learning and devotion.

Eastleigh and the Media

To speak of the media in relation to Eastleigh is a multi-faceted phenomenon. On the one level, one could map the place of Eastleigh in Kenyan media as a bastion of commerce and socialization and in recent past as an insecure neighbourhood, especially in the wake of increased grenade attacks. Secondly, Eastleigh exists at a meta-level as an extension of the Horn of Africa communities and, therefore, the residents are consumers and subjects of media from these regions. In the first level, the area features prominently in local radio, print and broad media as an enterprising niche for Somali business communities that have, over the years, built an economic empire that rivals 'indigenous' business elites. However, the area is featured regularly in the mainstream Kenyan media for the wrong reasons: as a den of 'sympathizers' of foreign-based militias out to settle scores with the Kenyan state and Kenyans for their armed participation in restoring peace in bordering Somali regions, an allegation that has fueled a xenophobic kind of distrust and suspicion and, in some cases, attacks against the largely diverse communities in the area. The media also frequently reports on multi-faith reconciliatory actions and increased measures of security, as well as the complex political competitions in the recent General Elections. Mainstream print and broadcast media, as well as faith-based and language-specific radios (e.g. Somali language FMs) and print media, report about Eastleigh on a regular basis.

Being an imagined extension of the Horn, Eastleigh is a hub for the broadcast and circulation of news, religious and non-religious media and advertised products from Kenya and neighbouring countries. It has been one of the most networked regions in Nairobi in terms of internet and mobile connectivity, ever since these services were in the formative stages of expansion in the country. This is largely due to the ever-increasing needs for connectivity for diasporic communication and commerce. Radio and television broadcasts from neighbouring states are often beamed into restaurants and homes via satellite dishes, giving exposure to local as well as foreign perspectives on the ongoing events in neighbouring countries and the

---

[38] It has been noted that diasporic membership is both status and identity which is relational, contextual and time-bound, and being in a Diaspora or, by extension, being in the city for many of the rural migrants, implies a tension between being in one place physically (the place where one lives and works) and thinking regularly of another place far away (Safran 2004). A core construction of Eastleigh as a place is the fragile notion of 'home' that could have been left by the first and subsequent generations through voluntary or involuntary displacements within and without the country. See also AvtarBrah (1996) on contesting diasporic identities and discourses.

world in a variety of languages.[39] Indeed, so engrained is Eastleigh in the commercial sphere of these diasporic enterprising communities and their broadcasts that television stations beamed via the satellites from neighbouring states prominently advertise Eastleigh's hotels, malls, hospitals and restaurants. That events such as the recent presidential elections in Somalia trigger jubilation in Eastleigh is proof of the multiple belongingness and consumption of media from outside Eastleigh.[40]

It is also worth noting that audio-visual media such as DVDs and VCDs on religious and non-religious themes massively circulate within Eastleigh. These materials are produced in various dialects of Somali, Amharic, Oromo, Arabic, Swahili and English. Such diverse forms of media in circulation strengthen diasporic networks and affirm simultaneous amorphous unity and fractures of the cultures of the greater Horn of Africa as imagined in the consumption patterns of Eastleighans.

To conclude, to think of Eastleigh is to think of many places, of many people and of many meanings that the place ascribes to itself and is ascribed to by others. Amidst the uncollected roadside garbage, unfinished roads, glittering shopping bazaars, spicy aromas of the rival restaurants, competing calls for departure for buses, loud announcements for prayers and hustle and bustle of traders and customers for bargains, a diverse community of people of various origins, cultures and religions compete to live and give meaning to their life. To these people, Eastleigh is everything. Media plays a pivotal role in shaping the imagination of this place for the locals and non-locals in equal measure.

Bibliography

Adamson, F. B. 2002."Mobilizing for the Transformation of Home: Politicized Identities and Transnational Practices", in Ali, NadjeSadig, and Khalid Koser (eds). *New Approaches to Migration?:Transnational Communities and the Transformation of Home.* London: Routledge.

Anderson, Benedict R. O. 1991. *Imagined communities: Reflections on the Origin and Spread of Nationalism.* Rev. and extended ed. London: Verso.

Brah, A. 1996.*Cartographies of Diaspora: Contesting Identities*. London: Routledge.

---

[39] When I moved to an apartment in the neighbourhood, I was surprised to find the new apartment already connected to a centralized digital cable television offering, among other channels, Barclays English premier leagues games; an assortment of local channels such as Citizen, Nation Television, Kenya Television Network; Aljezira English and Arabic; Ethiopian (ETV) and Eritrean national televisions; Bollywood's Zee TV, B4U; religious themed stations such as Iqra TV, Peace TV, Swahili language Africa TV-Swahili; Africa Magic for African movies; a few western movie channels; National Geographic and most conspicuously Somali language channels that broadcast news, music and religious programmes such as Somali National TV (SNTV), the Somali Channel, Universal TV, and Horn Cable TV (HCTV). For such an abundantly rich television menu, I was expected to pay 500 Kenyan Shillings (approximately 5 Euros) monthly. For about 12 Euros per month, one could also get connected to high speed cable internet connections and enjoy uninterrupted connectivity with the virtual world.

[40] Transnational migrant communities are increasingly interlinked with their home countries in a globalizing world and often engage in practices and strategies that facilitate or hinder political and social transformation and debates going on back home,. See F. B. Adamson (2002).

Mandaville, Peter G. 2001. *Transnational Muslim Politics: Reimagining the Umma.* London: Routledge.

Murunga, G. R. 2005. "'Inherently Unhygienic Races': Plague and the Origins of Settler Dominance in Nairobi, 1899–1907" in Salm, Steven J., and Toyin, Falola (eds). *African Urban Spaces in Historical Perspective.* Rochester: University of Rochester Press.

Obadare, E. and W. Adenbanwi. 2010. "The Visa God: Would-Be Migrants and the Instrumentalization of Religion" in Adogame, A. and J. V. Spickard (eds).*Religion Crossing Boundaries: Transnational Religious and Social Dynamics in Africa and the new African Diaspora.* Leiden: Brill.

Safran, W. 2004. "Deconstructing and Comparing Diasporas", in Kokot, Waltraud, Khachig Tölölyan, and Carolin Alfonso (eds). *Diaspora, Identity, and Religion: New Directions in Theory and Research.* London: Routledge.

White, Luise. 1990. *The Comforts of Home: Prostitution in Colonial Nairobi.* Chicago: University of Chicago Press.

CHAPTER THREE

Mapping Eastleigh as a Public Platform: The World of Street Preachers

Joseph Wandera[41]

Abstract

This contribution examines Muslim public preachers and their sermons in Eastleigh, Nairobi. It discusses how the preachers 'debate' with Christians. The preachers engage in open-air preaching (mihadhara) to dispute the teachings of Christianity and call Christians to embrace Islam. The article argues that public preaching as a form of engagement between Muslims and Christians has negative effects on relations between members of the two traditions. The contribution proposes an alternative model to the polemical debates in interfaith relations through Muslims' and Christians' engagement in joint action.

Background

Kenyan Muslims constitute a significant minority of between 10 to 15% of the total population (Oded, 200:1). In the last ten years, the public presence of Muslims has become more noticeable than hitherto. While this presence can be attributed to the global resurgence of religion in general and in Kenya in particular, it could also be traced back to various events in the recent past. These include the August 1998 twin bombings of the American Embassies in Nairobi and Dar-es-Salaam, which galvanized Muslims together amidst what they considered a 'negative' image of Islam portrayed in the media.

The other articles in this book by Willem Jansen, C.B. Peter and Halkano Abdi have demonstrated the various ways in which Muslims in Eastleigh are participating in the public space. Another important way through which Muslims are negotiating their place in the public square is through public preaching. I approach the phenomenon of public preaching from the perspective of religion in the public sphere. The notion of the public sphere is an important approach for analysing the contemporary revival of religion. This approach can be useful in explaining the resurgence of religion in the contemporary context in its complex and variant dimensions (Casanova, 1994). Tayob argues that "the role of religion in public life

---

[41]Joseph Wandera is a lecturer in the field of Islam and Christian-Muslim Relations and Religion and Public Life at St Paul's University, Kenya. With Willem Jansen, they founded and jointly manage the Centre for Christian-Muslim Relations in Eastleigh, (CCMRE) Nairobi on behalf of St Paul's University. This contribution is based on field work conducted at various periods between 2009-2013 for a larger Doctoral project submitted to the University of Cape Town, South Africa entitled: *Public Preaching by Muslims and Pentecostals in Mumias, Western Kenya and its Effects on Interfaith Relations*. The present contribution is based on data collected in Eastleigh, Nairobi.

seem[s] a more neutral approach to a complex and sensitive phenomenon" of religion that has dominated public life since the 1970s (Tayob, 2011:1). This theoretical approach is different from previous approaches that have examined religion from sociological and political dimensions. In locating Islam within the notion of religion in the public sphere, public Islam refers to a discourse within a new space (Muslim public) where ideas are presented and developed (Tayob, 2011:2). Such new spaces include open-air markets, streets and stadiums where public preaching takes place. In addition to locating the present study within the above theoretical framework, I approach public preaching in Eastleigh as forms of *da'wah*.[42] My approach in this contribution, thus, goes beyond the limitations of previous approaches on studying public Islam as *politics* or *economics* which are equally valid though limited considerations in the study of religion. The contribution seeks to reflect much more critically on public preaching as a religious practice within public Islam. By focussing on preaching and *da'wah*, I hope to extend the understanding of religion *qua* religion in the public sphere.

Public Preaching

Mihadhara (public preaching) is one of the most common religious phenomena in Eastleigh. A walk through this vast suburb will show various groups of Muslims staging their 'sermons' in different parts of the Estate. There is no single day that these activities are not taking place. There are various similarities and differences between the public sermons I studied in Mumias, Western Kenya and those presented in Eastleigh.[43] In both cases, these are public activities that are geared towards calling Christians to Islam. Moreover, in both places the preachers are mostly former Christians who converted to Islam. Therefore, the preachers have no formal training in religious sciences. Unlike the sermons in Mumias, sermons in Eastleigh are staged simultaneously by various preachers at various locations in this vast estate. Moreover, unlike similar events in Mumias that are held particularly in the afternoons, the preaching activities in Eastleigh take place at various times of the day between 10.00 am and 6.00 pm. While the audience at the events in Eastleigh is mostly composed of Muslims of Somali descent because of this demographic dominance in Eastleigh, in Mumias the audience is mainly composed of local *Wanga* Muslims.[44]

Although the sermons in Eastleigh are delivered mainly by Muslims based there, occasionally there are visiting preachers from other places such as Uganda and Tanzania. The sermons are a form of polemical *da'wah* in the style of Ahmed Deedat.[45] However the various preachers employ the Bible in a variety of ways. While some use the Bible to support Qur'anic positions, others are more emphatic in rejecting its validity.[46]

The attendance of Muslims at the preaching events in Eastleigh ranges between 200 and 500 people.[47] Unlike the sermons in Mumias, Western Kenya, which include significant publicity activities, for example using a public address system, the sermons in Eastleigh, except for the

---

[42] The term *da'wah* is the equivalent of the term mission in Christianity even though there are technical variations in the way the two terms are used.

[43] As earlier indicated, the author carried out a study of Muslim and Pentecostal public sermons in Mumias, Western Kenya as part of his doctoral work between 2009 and 2013.

[44] The *Wanga* is a sub-tribe of the larger Luhya tribe in Mumias, Western Kenya.

[45] Ahmed Deedat (1918-2005) was a well-known Muslim polemicist based in Durban, South Africa. He specialized in open–air debates with Christians in which he largely dismissed key doctrines of Christianity, arguing that Islam was the only valid religious tradition.

[46] This point was especially evident during my study of sermons in Mumias, Western Kenya.

[47] *Mihadhara* with a much higher attendance of up to 1000 people were occasionally staged at *Uhuru* park Nairobi, but these are staged approximately once per year.

initial invitation by the day's preacher through the public address, do not always have much prior publicity because of their regular nature. Both Muslims and Christians in Eastleigh are familiar with *mihadhara* as a part of their religious landscape. They know very well the venues and times when these events are held. The residents of Eastleigh also know the Muslim preachers. Many people in Eastleigh attend these preaching events as part of their daily routine. Moreover, Eastleigh is a place with a strong Muslim presence; hence there is no need to spend so much time calling out to Muslims and others to attend the events as is the case in Mumias, where the sermons are not held on a daily basis and Christians are many, hence the need for prior publicity.

The infrastructure and seating arrangement at an open air preaching is significant for how the sermon and debate is staged. There is always a table, a chair and a microphone for the person whose task is to audibly read both the Bible and Qur'ān. A Christian interlocutor, whenever there is one, sits on the opposite end of the Muslim reader of the various sacred texts. A moderator for the session is sandwiched between two Muslim preachers. He, too, has a microphone on the table in front of him. It is common to have two or three Muslim preachers taking turns to preach during one event. When no formal Christian interlocutor is present, the Muslim preacher tries to invite and/or goad one from the audience, sometimes successfully, at other times not. The polemical engagement between a Muslim and a Christian counterpart is an important part of the *mihadhara* as it contributes to its public appeal and its claim to be a form of outreach. Therefore, many preachers spend considerable effort to ensure that a "debate" is staged.

There is provision for seating for visiting *Imams* from local Mosques and prominent Muslim traders. The Christians stand in one corner of the preaching site while Muslims stand in the opposite direction. Women have a separate space reserved for them at a considerable distance from the men. They cover their heads with headscarves in accordance with Islamic norms. Some participants have pens and pieces of paper and make notes of the various Qur'anic and Biblical texts used by the preacher. The organizers also make sound recordings of the sermons for mass distribution. Sometimes Muslims sell compact discs (sold for 100 Kenyan shillings, or $1.25, in 2012). Other items like Qur'ans, white caps and prayer mats are also on sale.

A public address system is used to amplify the sermon. This device is powered by a small generator placed immediately behind the preacher. There are two or three big speakers strategically hoisted facing different directions. There is one microphone for the Islamic preacher, another for his Christian counterpart and a third for the reader of the Qur'ān.

Suleiman Mazinge, one of the preachers in Eastleigh, Nairobi [Photo by Joseph Wandera, 2010].

Effects of Sermons

Public preaching has on several occasions led to tension and violence in Eastleigh. Because of its approach, which is mainly adversarial and touching on the central doctrines of both Christianity and Islam, members of the audience are always tense and exhibit a negative attitude towards each other. In an interview with Abdurrahman Hassan he clearly explained the effects of these activities:

> Sometimes Muslims have exchanged bitter words with their Christian counterparts while preaching. I clearly remember in June 2005 when the exchange was so bitter that Muslims and Christians engaged in physical fights and the police had to intervene.[48]

The background to this incident is that during a preaching event a Christian interlocutor referred to the prophet Muhammed using derogatory words. The Muslims present shouted "*takbir*" leading to the ensuing fight.[49] On a different occasion, Joseph Ngola, a Christian interlocutor, posed a question to a Muslim preacher, which proved difficult for the Muslim to answer. According to Ngola, one Muslim from the audience stepped forward and slapped him hard on the cheeks. However, some Muslims in defence of Ngola intervened before a full scale fight between Muslims and Christians could begin.[50] The above two examples serve to show the adversarial nature of public preaching and its effects on how members of the two traditions relate to one another. These forms of engagement on many occasions force the intervention of the police to restore law and order.

---

[48] Interview with Abdulrahman Hassan, 22nd March 2013, Eastleigh.
[49] *Takbir* is the invocation of the religious incantation '*Allahu Akbar*' (God be praised). In the context of public preaching, this fomula is mostly used by Muslims when the preacher has said something which in the opinion of the Muslim audience is significant or a major score against the Christian interlocutor.
[50] Interview with Joseph Ngola, 29th March 2013, Eastleigh, Nairobi.

The Sermons

I will now examine three sermons preached in Eastleigh at various periods to demonstrate the various ways in which the preachers engaged in the public square. The first sermon was by Abdalla Ali, a young Muslim aged 29. He was born in a Christian family and converted to Islam while a student at a local secondary school. Ali stated that his attraction to Islam was caused by the "simplicity of the religion" unlike his previous tradition that contained difficult doctrines like the trinity. Ali began his preaching work first through an apprenticeship programme with one of the preachers before beginning to preach on his own much later. The second preacher was Suleiman Abdalla, also a former Christian from a Pentecostal tradition. Abdalla converted to Islam following a religious experience in which he was miraculously healed following prayers by a local Imam. He says that his engagement in preaching is a way of thanking Allah for the blessing of healing.[51] He was born in Kondele near Kisumu, Kenya, in a Christian family. The third preacher, Babu Salim, converted to Islam in 2001 following a dream in which he was shown a vision of Mecca with people engaged in *Salah* (prayer). After this experience, he visited a local Imam and requested to convert to Islam. He was then invited to recite the *Shahada* (the Islamic creed), effectively converting to Islam. Thereafter the preacher began listening to various public preachers who taught him how to preach as well.

'The Cross is cursed"- Ali

Abdalla Ali[52]'s sermon on 13th March, 2010 addresses the question of the significance of the cross. The broader context of Ali's sermon is his concern over what he sees as a satanic tradition called Free Masons and its presence in the public square. He explains to the audience that there are several symbols of the Free Masons Church. He explains these signs as: one eye found on the currency of the United States of America, three fingers which he argues the famous soccer player for the Brazilian National team, Ronaldino, flashes in salute whenever he scores a goal, a burning flame used during the Olympic Games and finally the cross. Without citing the specific Qur'anic chapter and verse, Ali states that Satan told God that he would go down upon the earth and mislead his people. Ali explains that such misleading of God's people includes telling people to eat animals that are *haram* (forbidden) such as pork, an obvious reference to Christians present. He then continues to explain that Satan informed God that he would dominate people's lives in all directions, "behind them, in front of them, on their right and on their left". This kind form of dominance, Ali explains, forms the cross, an important symbol in Christianity. Therefore, he argues that the cross is a satanic symbol as Satan clearly presented it before God as the manner in which he would dominate people's lives. Ali then gives a text from the Bible to back his arguments: "Christ redeemed us from the curse of the law by becoming a curse for us, for it is written: "cursed is everyone who is hung on a tree" (Galatians 3:13). In quoting this biblical text, Ali is solidifying his earlier argument based on the Qur'an that Satan made use of the symbol of the cross and, in a similar vein, the Bible presented the cross in a negative light. Based on this argument, Ali dismisses the Christian teaching that Jesus could have been crucified on the cross stating that: *"Ukiwekwa juu ya msalaba, wewe umelaaniwa kwa mjibu was Biblical"* (According to the Bible, you are cursed if you are hanged on the cross). At this point a Christian interlocutor called James Makokha raises his hand and is allowed to engage with Ali. He states that Ali is interpreting the Bible using his own understanding and that he is not

---

[51] Interview with Suleiman Abdallah, 29rd March 2013, Eastleigh, Nairobi.

[52] The names of the preachers have been changed to maintain their privacy as they have not been consulted about this article.

guided by the Holy Spirit. Ali responds by asking that Makokha provide an alternative interpretation. He also challenges Makokha to explain to the audience the nature of the Holy Spirit as it is another "confusing Christian doctrine". Makokha attempts to explain the meaning of the cross from a Christian perspective, arguing that what might appear to be a "curse" is actually redemptive in Christian belief. Ali quickly responds that, this is simply a human idea (*zana*) and has no basis in scripture. He challenges Makokha to give a biblical text to back his assertions while Makokha requests to be given more time to find a text. "*Takbir,*" shouts Ali to which all Muslims respond "Allah *Akbar*". Christians, he argues, do not have enough *elimu* (education) and need to go back to school.

"Do not Mix Men and Women in Mourning"- Abdallah

The second sermon that I will examine was preached by Suleiman Abdallah on 29th March 2013 on 9th Street in Eastleigh. In his sermon, Abdallah argues that it is wrong for Christians to mix males and females during public events such as funerals and worship. He bases his argument on Zechariah 12:11-14 in which context people are moaning but with the two genders separated from one another. He asks the reader to read the text:

> On that day the weeping in Jerusalem will be great, like the weeping of Hadad Rimmon in the plain of Megiddo. The land will mourn, each clan by itself, with their wives by themselves: the clan of the house of David and their wives, the clan of the house of Nathan and their wives, the clan of the house of Levi and their wives, the clan of Shimei and their wives, and all the rest of the clans and their wives.

Based on this reading, Abdalla argues that there should be proper decorum in mourning, characterised with separation of males and females. "You might be mourning here, and there is someone's wife next to you. If a female's thigh is next to yours, there will no longer be mourning but something else". Abdallah argues that whenever Muslims advocate for such religious decorum, they are accused of discriminating against women. He challenges Christians, stating that if they did not separate the two genders in funerals and worship, God would punish them as his teaching on this matter was clearly in the Bible.

"Jesus worshipped in a Mosque not a Church; emulate him"- Salim

Babu Salim preached on 7th Street Eastleigh on 10th April 2013 on the above theme. He begins his sermon by inviting a Christian to engage with him. The first Christian, Emmanuel, refuses to step forward for the engagement despite repeated appeals by Salim to do so. Eventually another Christian called Andrew is persuaded to come forward. Salim then proceeds: "Andrew Nganyi you are a Christian, I am a Muslim. The Muslim believes in Jesus, so does the Christian. Why then do they worship in different places?" Nganyi argues that during the times of Jesus, he did not worship in a specific place as he was an itinerant preacher. "Are you telling us that Jesus never entered a Church?" asks Salim. This time round, Nganyi states that Jesus' church was a synagogue. Salim then challenges Nganyi that if anyone today is seen worshipping in a church, he is not a true follower of Jesus. He challenges Nganyi to read a text from a Kiswahili Bible in Luke 4:16 which translates the meaning of synagogue as "Jewish Mosque". On the basis of this translation, Salim then argues again that Jesus worshipped in a Mosque not a Church. Nganyi agrees with him. "I go to the Mosque and you attend the Church; who is following Jesus?" Salim asks. He quotes Matthew 12:30, which states that whoever is not with me is against me, to argue that the fact that Christians do not go to Mosques like Jesus did demonstrates that they do not follow Jesus.

Some Characteristics of Eastleigh Sermons

There are some salient features about the sermons that one can identify. From their Christian past, all the preachers extensively use the Bible in varied ways. All the preachers use the Bible to support their arguments. Such preachers interpret the Bible from Qur'anic perspectives. Second, in their attempts to use the Bible, the preachers' plans are disrupted by Christian interlocutors who present objections to the preachers' use of textual sources and offer alternative interpretations. Sometimes the interlocutors demand "evidence" from different textual sources. At other times they completely reject the interpretations given. They also challenge the preachers' positions, citing historical evidence. Most of these engagements end without a clear "victor" in the debate. However, it is important to recognize that Muslim public preaching is a staged debate, reflected in the setting of the scene, the placing of interlocutors, and the call by Muslims to argue debate and prove themselves.

The preachers also use various rhetorical approaches. This is not surprising given the very long duration of these public encounters. They repeat verses of the Bible and the Qur'an as they were read in public. Through using such repetitions, the preachers are able to emphasize certain points that they wish to make. They also sing Christian songs to match their appeal to Biblical texts. While singing, they change their voices and body movement to emphasize certain points. The preachers engage with the audience, asking them to argue. The preachers also rely on the audience for support as they publicly call out "*Takbir*" (lit. "To make [God] great") and the Muslim audience respond "*Allah Akbar*" ("God is great!").

In summary, public preachers in Eastleigh and their sermons represent new religious authorities. All the preachers I interviewed are former Christians who strive to occupy a position of authority in society. Their claim to authority is based on their religious experiences. The preachers' religious encounters are varied but all impact on their decisions to begin preaching. The preachers use their knowledge and experience of Christianity to make a claim for the superiority of Islam on the basis of the Bible. While more orthodox Islamic preachers would support their arguments by relying on an authoritative discursive tradition where their sources would be the Qur'an and *Hadith*, the sermons demonstrate how these preachers are attempting to find a foundation on the Bible for Islamic arguments. As former Christians, they use the Bible easily to support their positions, with liberal references to the Qur'an. The main foundation is the Bible, even though the theology is Islamic. Some of the preachers are more active opponents of the Biblical narratives relating to Jesus, but repeatedly return to the Bible to support their Islamic arguments. In their attempts to achieve this goal, the public preachers encounter Christian interlocutors who ask questions and challenge their use of textual sources. However, the Muslim preachers overcome this challenge through staged events using various rhetorical means. In their staging of their sermons, they use the Bible, Christian beliefs and songs. This approach proves effective in their work, even though their Christian interlocutors and many in the audience remain unconvinced.

Finally, the public sermons are staged as debate and contestations. They set up the public preaching places as debating rooms, where preachers, supporters and opponents take their place. They then frame questions for debate, and produce evidence to prove their point. Irrespective of the merits of their argument, it is important to recognize how *da'wah* in this manifestation is a form of public duel. There are elements of self-renewal evident, but the dominant approach is marked by debate, competition and contestation.

Towards Diapraxis as a Model for Interfaith Engagement

It is no longer sufficient for religious traditions to merely talk about their respective beliefs. This is especially so when such talking is polemical, leading to tension and violence. It is against this background that the Centre for Christian–Muslim Relations in Eastleigh (CCMRE) encourages Muslims and Christians to engage in joint action on matters of common concern in order to enhance peaceful co-existence. In the Project Report by CB Peters (Chapter Six), he describes mapping as an example of joint action between Muslims and Christians. The centre is also involved in other activities such as praying for peace during the 2013 election in Kenya, and drawing joint statements in the face of increased incidents of insecurity in Eastleigh. In this way CCMRE has rearticulated interfaith engagement, referring not so much anymore to 'dialogue' but to 'diapraxis', the practical reality of living and working together with Muslims. This approach is based on the realisation that we need to be in contact with each other and to experience one another as human beings. This approach towards interfaith engagement is not totally new to the African context which has a long tradition of Christians and Muslims living together in harmony, even among same families.

Conclusion

This contribution has demonstrated that public preaching is an important way through which Muslims are engaging in the public square in Eastleigh. The nature of this engagement is polemical and confrontational, leading to tension and violence between Muslims and Christians. At the Centre for Christian-Muslim Relations in Eastleigh, we attempt to offer a different model of engagement between Muslims and Christians. This approach mainly involves Muslims and Christians engaging in joint projects such as mapping, environmental conservation and advocacy. We believe that better relations between members of various religions are best achieved through such joint ventures and not so much through debates.

Eastleigh as a Public Platform: Posters such as above often adorn the streets of Eastleigh inviting Christians and Muslims to public debates. Willem Jansen appears in the above poster.[Photo: Willem Jansen]

Bibliography

Casanova, J. 1994. *Public religions in the modern world.* Chicago: University of Chicago Press.

Oded, A. 1996. Islamic Extremism in Kenya: The Rise and Fall of Sheikh Khalid Balala. *Journal of Religion in Africa.* 26(4):406-15pp.

Lewis, IM. 1994. *A Modern History of the Somali: Nation and State in the Horn of Africa* (4th ed.), Oxford: James Curry.

Nielsen, J.S. 1999. Towards a European Islam, Houndsmills, Basingstroke: Hampshire.

Tayob, A. 2012.Politics and Islamization in African Public Spheres. *Islamic Africa*, Vol 3:2, 139-168pp.

Trimingham, J, Spencer. 1965. *Islam in Ethiopia.* London: Oxford University Press.

CHAPTER FOUR

A Street Preacher's Da'wah

Ibrahim Issack

*The contribution below was solicited from a public preacher in Eastleigh. The views expressed do not represent the position of the Centre for Christian-Muslim Relations (CCMRE). However, we hope the reader will find the contribution useful in terms of providing some insights on how the preachers view their activities. [**Editors**]*

Islamic public preaching in Eastleigh, Nairobi is an initiative of 8th Street Da'wah Group which was formed over nineteen years ago by a number of people who had been doing comparative religious research together. Out of the eight founding members, only two were born Muslims while the other six are former Christians and Pastors who reverted to Islam and decided to share their newfound truth with an urge to save the world from false religions and cults.

Salim Ndeda, one of the converts, started preaching to the non-Muslims at 8th Street Eastleigh 1st Avenue. Eventually, the number of preachers grew to the eight people that later saw the first open air comparative da'wah at 8th Street, 1st Avenue, Eastleigh.

Despite the challenges from both Muslims and Christians who were not accustomed to this new kind of preaching in their surroundings, the preachers stood firm and defended their cause for the sake of Allah. The group has witnessed tremendous success and achievements towards reaching thousands in Kenya and Africa as a whole. With this growth at hand they started targeting international avenues where the message of Islam had not reached to the non-Muslims. In this endeavor the preachers have been able to reach out to non-Muslims in South Africa, Democratic Republic of Congo, Zambia, Rwanda, Burundi, Uganda, Botswana, Ghana, Nigeria, Angola, and Zimbabwe and are still aiming for the entire African continent and the world. In the last thirteen years over 10,000 people have reverted to Islam through their da'wah endeavor.

Comparative da'wah is fully backed up by both the Bible and the Qur'an. For example, the book of Hosea 4:6 states that "my people are destroyed from lack of knowledge". Further, in Acts 15:21 it is stated that "For Moses of old time hath in every city them that preach him, being read in the synagogues every Sabbath day". In the Qur'an every believer has been given the mantle to call all mankind to monotheism, as we read in the Qur'an Surah Al-Imran (3) 60-64.

CHAPTER FIVE

A Sūfī Perspective on Christian-Muslim Relations in Eastleigh and Beyond

Sūfī Merabaqsh Abdul-Aziz Bunni

Abstract

In Eastleigh and the neighbouring estate of Pumwani, sufism[53] is widely practiced. The sūfī brotherhoods represent the majority of Muslims in Eastleigh and Pumwani. The Brotherhoods, spread throughout the streets of the estates, are comprised of many turūq (sūfī orders, or brotherhoods) such as Qadiriya, Shadhiliya and Da'watil Islami from Pakistan. Yet, the wider world seems hardly to be aware of this mystical dimension of Islam. In this article, therefore, the existence of this rather unknown world of Eastleigh will be presented. From a rights-based perspective in Islam, the question is discussed of how sūfīs think about Christian-Muslim relations in Eastleigh and beyond.

Introduction

"In the name of Allah, the most gracious, the most merciful",
All praise is due to Allah, Lord of the universe, and peace and blessing be upon our Messenger Muhammad Bin Abdullah (*peace and blessing of Allah be upon Him*, P.B.U.H), and upon his descendants and companions.

Islam is the religion of mercy to all people. The Lord says in the Holy Qur'an, *"These are clear evidences to men, a guidance and mercy to those of assured faith"* (Al-Jathiyah, 45: 20).There is goodness in Islam for all living beings for those who believe in it, and for non-Muslims as well. This fact can be ascertained by anyone with insight, and only someone who is arrogant or ignorant of the realities of Islam could deny its virtue. The Lord says, *"That is the true religion but most among mankind know not"* (Ar-Rum 30: 30).

It is very important, with regard to Muslim-Christian relations, to learn these important verses of the Holy Qur'an and Ahadiths (traditions) of the Holy Prophet (P. B. U. H.).Anyone who is familiar with works of *fiqh* (Islamic Law), knows that Muslim scholars of *fiqh* use the

---

[53]Here I have to explain some terminology of Sufism (mysticism). A *sūfī* (mystic) is a member of a Muslim group who tries to become united with the Almighty God through prayer and meditation, and by living a very simple and strict life. So without explaining a few *ayās* (verses), I will not have explained in detail about a devoted Muslim sufi-member, who is obviously part of *Ahli Sunna Wal Jamaa*,specifically from the *Ahli Twarika*. As a *sūfī*, you must be attending *dhikri* (remembrance) *maulīd* (celebration of the birth of the Prophet), *du'a* (public supplication) and many occasions of *Ahli Twarika*. It is actually not *bid'a* (innovation) or *haram* (forbidden). We have the full support of some verses of the Holy Qur'an and *ahadiths* (traditions) of our beloved Prophet (P. B.U.H.) and also from the *ijma'* (consensus) of our scholars of *Ahlu Sunna wal Jamaa* and from the *Ahli Twarika*.

technical term "people of the covenant" (*dhimmi*), to refer to citizens who are non-Muslims. It is an attractive term and not a pejorative one as some would claim. It means "the people of testament and trust", because they are under the protection of the covenant, extended to them by the Prophet Muhammad (P.B.U.H.) and Muslims. This covenant is valid forever[54]. We should respect our neighbours and non-Muslim relatives. To be a devoted Muslim, one must know and respect the rights of non-Muslims everywhere. It is very important to have positive Muslim-Christian relations in all aspects.

The Dignity of All Humanity

Every Muslim must know the rights of non-Muslims, their right to the preservation of their dignity as human beings. Almighty Allah has endowed mankind with dignity, Muslims and non-Muslims alike, and has elevated humanity's status above that of much of the creation. The Almighty says in the Holy Qur'an,

> *We have honoured the sons of Adam; provided them with transport on land and sea; given them for sustenance things good and pure; and conferred on them special favours, above a great part of our creation. (Banī Al-Isra'il 17: 70)*

The Almighty Allah even commanded His angels to prostrate themselves in humility before Adam, the father of mankind (P.B.U.H.). This command was to elevate the status and honour of humanity. The Almighty Allah also said, when He addressed the angels, "*Prostrate yourselves to Adam; they prostrated themselves, but not Iblīs, he refused*" (*Taha* 20: 116).

The Almighty Allah, (*subhana wattaala*, Glory be to God), bestowed many favors upon mankind, some of which are evident, and others which are hidden. He made the heavens and earth subject to man as a sign of his honour. The Almighty Allah says in the Holy Qur'an,

> *It is Allah who hath created the heavens and the earth and sendeth down rain from the skies, and with it bringeth out fruits wherewith to feed you; it is he who hath made the ships subject to you that they may sail through the sea by his command; and the rivers (also) hath he made subject to you and he giveth you of all that ye ask for, but if ye count the favors of Allah, never will ye be able to number them. Verily man is given up to injustice and ingratitude (Ibrahīm 14: 32-34)*

It is very important to know that as a devoted Muslim, one should respect other human beings, especially the non-Muslims. Also it is very important to have good manners and seek knowledge. Those are very essential issues which can make you succeed in the world and in the life after death. The Holy Prophet (P.B.U.H.) says: "*The person nearest to me on the Day of Judgment will be he, whose manners are excellent and who is humblest in his behavior towards mankind*"[55]. Another Hadith says, "*A person who acts without knowledge is likely to do more harm than good*". This elevated status that Almighty Allah (*suhanahu wataala*) has granted to mankind is the basis for the principle of preservation of human dignity, regardless of whether a person is Muslim or Non-Muslim, and it is hard to imagine any religion that can equal Islam in its preservation of human dignity for all.

---

[54] Az-Zahili W. *Islam and Non-Muslims*: 60-62.
[55] Compare *Sahīh Buchari*: 506.

Islam emphasizes that the origin of mankind is one, and therefore all humanity has equal rights. Allah (*suhanahu wataala*) has said,

> *Mankind! We created you from a single (pair) of a male and female and made you into nations and tribes, that ye may know each other (Not that ye may despise each other). Verily the most honored of you in the sight of Allah is (he who is) the most righteous of you. And Allah has full knowledge and is well Acquitted (with all things) (Al-Hujurāt 49: 13)*

The Messenger of Allah, (P.B.U.H.) said in his sermon during the days of *tashrīq* (celebration of the *'īd)*, the pilgrimage in the tenth year of the *Hijrah,*"People, hear that your Lord is one, and that your father is one. You must know that an Arab has no superiority over a non–Arab, or a non-Arab over an Arab, or a Redman over a Black man, or a Black over a Red, except in terms of what each possesses in piety. Have I delivered the message?"[56] An example of the preservation of the dignity of non-Muslims is their right to respect for their feelings and to mannerly speech in debate, in obedience to the command of Allah:

> *And dispute ye not with the people of the book, except in the best way, unless it be with those of them who do wrong, but say, "We believe in the revelation which has come down to us and in that which came down to you; our God and your God is one; and it is to him we submit (in Islam) (Al-'Ankabūt 29: 46)*

Respect for the Beliefs of Non-Muslims

Non-Muslims have the right to not have their beliefs mocked. I do not believe there is a religion or sect on the face of the earth that is more just in regard to those who have other beliefs than Islam. Is it not true that Allah has said in the Holy Qur'an,

> *Say: who gives you sustenance from the heavens and the earth? Say: it is Allah; and certain it is that either we or ye are on right guidance or in manifest error (Sabā' 34: 24).*

Allah has honoured mankind to the point that He has forbidden Muslims to speak badly of the deities worshipped by polytheists, so that the polytheists are not led to speaking badly of Allah the one God. This is an example of the honoured rank of a person, because respect for the feelings of a person towards that which he holds sacred, is a form of respect for his dignity. So the words of the Almighty Allah on this topic are,

> *Revile ye not those whom they call upon beside Allah, lest they out of spite revile Allah in their ignorance. This we have made alluring to each people its own doings. In the end will they return to their Lord and he shall then tell them the truth of all that they did (Al-An'ām 6: 108)*

In another example of the principle of human dignity, the prophet Muhammad (P.B.U.H.) narrated, "The Prophet stated, "When you see a funeral, you must stand until it has passed you by"[57]. On another occasion the following happened, "One day a funeral procession passed by and the Prophet (S.A.W) stood up. The people objected, "But it is the funeral of a Jew", and He the Prophet responded, "Is he not a human being?"[58] So again, being a devoted Muslim you should totally respect the rights to freedom of non-Muslims.

---

[56] *Musnad al-Imam Ahmad*, Vol. 12: 226.
[57] *Sahīh al-Bukhari*, Vol. 2: 86.
[58] Idem.

Islam has never compelled those who do not agree with it to convert. It has declared their complete freedom to retain their own faith, and to not be forced to embrace Islam. This freedom is documented in both the Qur'an and in the Ahadith of the Holy Prophet Muhammad (S.A.W.). *"It had been the Lord's will, they would all have believed, all of who are on earth; wilt thou then compel mankind against their will, to believe!"* (Yūnus 10: 99). Our Prophet (S.A.W.) used to give people a choice between entering Islam and retaining their current religion.

These directives of the prophet Muhammad (S.A.W.) are in obedience to the word of the Almighty: *"Let there be no compulsion in religion, truth stands out clear from error: who ever rejects Taghut and believes in Allah hath grasped the most trustworthy hand-hold that never breaks and Allah heareth and knoweth all things"* (al-Baqarah 2: 256-257).

This is the same verse of the Qur'an which was explained by an American Scholar, Edwin Calgary as follows, "There is a noble verse in the Qur'an that is filled with truth and wisdom, and it is known to all Muslims. Everyone else should know it as well; it is the one that says there is no compulsion in religion".[59] So every Muslim should take in mind that nobody is allowed to underrate anybody or force anybody to join his sect. Our work is only preaching the message and, most importantly, keeping good relations with your neighbours.

You can perform your *salāt* (prayer) and fasting and other pillars of Islam, but if you do not have respect for neighbours and people of other religions, you fail to enter paradise. So let us fear Allah so that we can enter *jannah* (garden, paradise). The Lord has said in the Holy Qur'an,

> *Say, "The truth is from you Lord, Let him who will believe, and let him who will, reject it. For the wrong-doers we have prepared a fire whose (smoke and flames) like the wall and roof of a tent, will hem them in: if they implore relief they will be granted water like melted brass, that will scald their faces how dreadful the drink: how uncomfortable a couch to recline on!"* (*Al-Kahf* 18: 29).

Islam does not only give freedom of religious affiliation to non-Muslims. Its tolerant law extends to facilitating their worship services and preserving their places of worship. The Almighty Allah (*subhanahu wataala*) has said in the Holy Qur'an,

> *They are those who have been expelled from their homes in defiance of right (for no cause) except that they say, "Our Lord is Allah." Did not Allah check one set of people by means of another there would surely have been pulled down monasteries, churches, synagogues, and mosques, in which the name of Allah is commemorated in abundant measure. Allah will certainly aid those who aid His (cause); for verily Allah is full of strength, exalted in might (Able to enforce His will)* (*Al-Hajj* 22: 40).

The Just Treatment of Non-Muslims

Islam is clear in minding the non-Muslims' right to justice. Islam is the religion of justice; Allah (*subhana wataala*) has demanded that we use a just measure in all affairs, so everyone acts equitably, and is cautious to not fall into oppressive ways. The Almighty Allah said:

---

[59] Calgary E. *The Near-East: Society and Culture: 163-164.*

> *And the firmament has He raised high, and He has set up the balances (of justice), ye may not transgress (due) balance. So establish weight with justice and fall not short in the balance (Ar-Rahmān 55: 7-10).*

The Almighty Allah ordered Muslims to act equitably in all matters, even if equity means a loss to themselves or to those closest to them, as is stated in this verse:

> *O ye who believe! Stand out firmly for justice and as witnesses to Allah, even as against yourselves, or your parents, or your kin and whether it be (against) rich or poor: for Allah can best protect both. Follow not the lusts (of your hearts), lest ye swerve, and if ye distort (justice) or decline to do justice, verily Allah is well – acquainted with all that ye do (An-Nisāa 4: 135).*

So here we have another important teaching on the human rights of non–Muslims, "*Namely, that no bearer of burden can bear the burden of another*" (*An –Najm* 53: 38). The most compelling of the commandments of the Prophet (S.A.W.) to preserve and follow is when He said, "*If anyone oppresses a dhimmī (non-Muslim) or burdens him with something too great for him, I will argue against him (the oppressor[60]). They are not slaves, which would make it permissible to move them from one country to another. They are free people of the covenant*".

The justice Islam offers to non-Muslims in every time and place is unparallel in other religions, nations or governments. Scholars and statesmen from the world over, have left record of their recognition of this fact in history books, so others can realize the truth. The famous British historian, H. G. Wells wrote the following about the teachings of Islam:

> They established greater traditions of just interaction. They inspire people with a spirit of generosity and tolerance, and are humanitarian and practical. They created a human community in which it was rare to see cruelty and social injustice, unlike any community that came before it[61].

In contrast, Sir Thomas Arnold discusses he strife between feuding Christian sects, who were always at each other's throats during the first centuries of Islamic rule[62].

Islam protects basic human rights for all people. These rights include preservation of the life of person, property and honour. Muslims and non-Muslims are equal in this right. Whether they are citizens or visitors, these are sacred rights that are carefully guarded, and cannot be abrogated for any reason except by law. It is not permissible to kill a non-Muslim unless he is sentenced for murder of a capital crime, because the Almighty Allah has said,

> *Say, "I come, I will rehearse what Allah hath (really) prohibited you from: join not anything as equal with him; be good for your parents, kill not your children on a plea of want. We provide sustenance for you and for them. Come not night to shameful deeds whether open or secret; take not life, which Allah hath made sacred, except by way of justice and law: thus doth He command you, that ye may learn wisdom (Al-An'ām 6: 151).*

---

[60]*As-Sunnah al-Kubra lil-Bayhaqi*, Vol. 9: 205.
[61]As-Suba'i, M. 1999 *Splendors of Our Civilization*: 146.
[62]Arnold T. 1970*Invitation to Islam*: 87-88.

Again the Almighty Allah has said,

> On that account: We ordained for the children of Israel that if any one slew a person unless it be for murder or for spreading mischief in the land it would be as if he slew the whole people and if any one saved a life, it would be as if he saved the life of the whole people (Al-Mā'idah 5: 32).

Our prophet Muhammad (S.A.W.) said in His sermon on the day Arafah, "*Your blood, your property and your honor are all sacred as sacred as this (Holy) day of yours, your city, and this (sacred) month*"[63]. This sanctity is not for Muslims alone, because the Prophet (S. A.W.) also said, "*Whoever kills a person with whom we have a treaty, will not even come close enough to paradise to smell its scent, and its scent can be found at a distance of forty years of travel*"[64].

It is not permissible to harm a non-Muslim without cause in any manner, such as violating his honour, transgressing against his property, assaulting him or killing him without legal right. It has even been recorded in more than one source that one of the Muslims killed a man from the people of the covenant, and the case was brought before the prophet Muhammad (S.A.W.) who said, "*I am the one most obligated to fulfill his covenant*", and ordered the murderer to be executed[65].

Every devoted Muslim should know non-Muslims' right to protection from aggression: One of the rights of non-Muslims that cannot be taken lightly is that Muslims must protect any of them living in their territory from any external enemy who wishes to do them harm, since they have the general rights of any Muslim citizen. Their payment of the *jizyah* (polltax) entitles them to protection from harm, defense against any aggression, and ransom of any of them who are taken as prisoners by an enemy. To abandon the protection of non-Muslim subjects would be a severe form of oppression, and Islam is a religion that combats all form of oppression. The Almighty Allah said in the Holy Qur'an, "*And whoever among you does wrong, him shall We cause to taste of a grievous penalty*" (Al Furqān 25: 19).

The Messenger of Allah the Prophet Muhammad (S.A.W.) stated that Allah has declared in a *Hadith Qudsi*, "*O My servants! I have made oppression forbidden to Myself, and I have made it forbidden between you, so do not oppress*".

A devoted Sufi Muslim should clearly know the non–Muslims' right to good treatment. The Qur'an is the venerated basis for interrelations with non-Muslims, and it has made clear that they must be treated well. Interactions must be based on charity and generosity of spirit as long as non-Muslims do not show overt hostility to us. Allah Almighty has said,

> Allah forbids you with regard to those who fight you not for (your) faith nor drive you out of your homes, from dealing kindly and justly with them: For Allah loveth those who are just. Allah only forbids you with regard to those who fight you for (your) faith, and drive you out of your homes, and support (others) on driving you out, from turning to them (for friendship and protection) it is such (Muslims) as turn to them that do wrong (Al-Mumtahinah 60: 8-9).

---

[63] *Sahih al Bukhari* Vol. 2: 191.
[64] *Sunah ad-Daru Qutni*, Vol. 3: 135; Hadith no. 168.
[65] *Sahih Bukhari*, Vol. 8: 48.

So in all these verses, "dealing kindly" has a meaning much greater than "good treatment", being much deeper and more inclusive.

Generosity Towards Non-Muslims

The companions of the Prophet Muhammad (S.A.W.) followed his magnanimous example in their treatment of non-Muslims. The commander of the faithful, 'Umar ibn al-Khatab (*radhia lahu anhu*, may Allah be pleased with him) ordered that a regular stipend be set up from the treasury for the benefit of a Jewish family to whom the Prophet (P.B.U.H.) had given charity. He justified His decision to allot funds for the People of the Book by referring to the verse of the Qur'an where the Almighty Allah states,

> *Alms are for the poor and the needy, and those employed to administer (the funds): for those whose hearts have been (recently) reconciled (to truth); for those in bondage and in debt; in the cause of Allah; and for the Wayfarer: (Thus is it) ordained by Allah. And Allah is full of knowledge and wisdom (At-Taubah 9: 60).*

A number of unbiased western historians have attested to the Holy Prophet Muhammad's (S. A. W.) generous spirit that has characterized the Muslims, that is, their kind treatment of non-Muslims. Renault wrote, "The Muslims in the cities of al-Andalus treated the non-Muslim in the best possible fashion. In return, the non-Muslims should respect the sensibilities of the Muslims and would circumcise their children, and refrain from eating pork"[66]. Another important act to a SufiMuslim is to mind the right to social security of non-Muslims. The *fukkara* (poor) refers to Muslims and the *masakīn* (needy) refers to the people of the book such as the *ayah* says (*At-Tawbah* 9:60).

Thus, *swahaba* (companion of the Prophet) 'Umar (*radhia'alahu anhu*) orderd that *jizyah* not to be collected from an old man from the non-Muslims. When the commander of the faithful, 'Umar Bin al-Khatwab (*may Allah be pleased with him*) was visiting Damascus, he passed by a group of Christian amputees. He ordered that they be given money in charity and have stipends established to provide them with food. Another similar order was written by the commander of the Muslims, 'Umar bin Abdul-Aziz (*may Allah have mercy on him*) to Adiy Ibn Anta'ah, his agent in al-Basra, "Seek out any of the people of the covenant in your area who have grown old and weak and are unable to earn money, and establish stipends for them from the treasury to provide for their needs".

Some of the successors used to distribute part of the *zakāt al-fitri* (the obligatory charity at the end of *ramadhān*) to Christian monks, based on their understanding of the verses of the Qur'an, that comments on distribution of *zakāt* and who is supposed to get the share (*Al-Mumtahinah* 60:8).

Christian-Muslim Relations in Eastleigh

Maintaining peace and good human relations is very important to both Christians and Muslims. To have good relations, both in this country and all over the world, there must exist community-based groups who can join Christians and Muslims in relationships. So *masha'allah*, St. Paul's University has a special programme on Muslim-Christian relations, withthe brave and intelligent Mr. Willem Jansen. Mr. Jansen and his faculty also have a

---

[66] As-Suba'I 1999: 147

Centre at Eastleigh on Eighth Street, called CCMRE, in the Eastleigh Fellowship Centre (Mennonite). We have activities of Muslim-Christian relations there, so may the Almighty reward Mr. Willem Jansen and Mr. Joseph Wandera for their marvelous work at the University and also at the Fellowship Center in Eastleigh. As Christians or as Muslims, people must take seriously these activities and the human rights relations which we are working on. Our main aim is to have peace in this country and also to build bridges. Another important goal of our activities is to uplift the standard of education from secondary level to university. I started two government schools, one in Nairobi and the other at Ngara. Our main aim is to help the community and also uplift the standard of education in the communities of Eastleigh, Mathare and Majengo Pumwani.

So, concluding my contribution on the rights of non-Muslims in Islam, since I was born here in Eastleigh 54 years ago, there have been good Muslim-Christian relations. The neighbours and the community in general used to share and respect each other's faiths with neighbours and non-Muslim relatives. It is therefore our duty as the Holy Books are guarding us, to have good relations and to pay respect and have mercy for each other so that peace and harmony can prevail in our country and every part of the world. Even though at present there are forces against us, the Almighty will guide us. By working together with St. Paul's University and the Centre for Christian-Muslim relations in Eastleigh, it is our duty to enjoin the community in Eastleigh and beyond.

It's me, your brother,
Merabaqsh Abdul-Aziz Bunni

CHAPTER SIX

Mapping Eastleigh for Christian-Muslim Relations: A Project Report

C. B. Peter

> 'What the map ultimately charts, in other words,
> is nothing less than the contours of the human experience itself:
> the never-ending attempt to imagine a place for ourselves in the world.'[67]
> -Toby Lester

Abstract

This chapter explores the option of studying Eastleigh spatiality jointly by Christians and Muslims as a "lived experience" and understanding together how mapping the commonly shared space can enhance our insights into Christian-Muslim relations. Twelve teams of mappers consisting of one Christian and one Muslim each mapped the 12 streets in Section 1 of Eastleigh, Nairobi between November 15 and 17, 2012. Their approach to mapping was phenomenological, i.e. mapping the Eastleigh spatiality as a "lived experience" and then seeing together how such an approach could help understand Christian-Muslim relations in Eastleigh better and in a more positive and optimistic perspective. The insights generated from this project had a transformative impact on the mappers, both in their self-perceptions as well as their perceptions of Christian-Muslim relations.

Introduction

Christian-Muslim relationship is an issue of immense socio-economic and security-related implications for Africa, Asia, the Middle East, and other parts of the world. St. Paul's University in Limuru, Kenya has a twofold approach to understand and improve this relationship: (1) a department of Islam and Christian-Muslim Relations (ICMR) offering a residential MA degree programme, and (2) a Centre for Christian Muslim Relations in Eastleigh (CCMRE), operating in the eastern suburb of Nairobi. The area, largely dominated by Somali Muslims, is a hub of economic activity running 24 hours, Monday to Sunday.

It appears that Christian-Muslim relations in our times may be characterized by three major paradigms. One is that of peaceful co-existence in a secular regime, as is the case in India. The second is the extreme paradigm of Christian-Muslim political hostility and perpetual wars, as is the case in Nigeria. The third is somewhere in between the two—an apparently peaceful co-existence on the one hand and an underlying mutual suspicion and hostility on the other. Such hostility manifests itself in frequent public debates in the name of interfaith

---

[67]Toby Lester in reference to the Waldseemuller Map (1507), the oldest map to date mentioning 'America.' Toby Lester, *The Fourth Part of the World* (New York: Free Press, 2009), 398.

dialogues, often ending in violence. Such is the case with Eastleigh as ably demonstrated in Dr. Wandera's Chapter 3 in this book.

The Eastleigh mapping project, which I am reporting in the present chapter, sought to explore a fourth option—studying Eastleigh spatiality jointly by Christians and Muslims as a "lived experience" and understanding together how mapping the commonly shared space can enhance our insights about Christian-Muslim relations.

In November 2012, CCMRE carried out a three-day mapping exercise in Eastleigh in relation to Christian-Muslim relations. The present chapter contains a report of that exercise.

The cutting edge of our mapping approach was that more than constructing maps of the Eastleigh space, we were interested in the mapping behaviour itself and how such behaviour can impact on our own perceptions, especially with regards to Christian-Muslim relations. The underlying hypothesis in such an approach was that an existential and phenomenological engagement with place can have a transformative impact on our earlier perceptions. As Toby Lester in the epigraph to the present chapter observes, a map is not merely an objectively drawn picture of a place; it actually represents "the contours of human experience itself." Thus we were not so much interested in mapping the Eastleigh space as a dispassionately-observed reality, but in studying the space as a "lived experience" of people—Christians and Muslimsobserving what lessons such engagement can teach us about Christian-Muslim relations in Eastleigh, and by extension elsewhere. Such an approach in the present study has been called "the phenomenological approach" to mapping.

STATEMENT OF THE PROBLEM
The present mapping project was carried out to seek answers to the following questions:
1. What bearing does space as "observed reality" have on Christian-Muslim relations in Eastleigh?
2. What bearing does space as "lived experience" have on Christian-Muslim relations in Eastleigh?
3. In what way does our existential engagement with space and place impact on our perceptions?
4. What lessons can be learnt from mapping for Christian-Muslim relations?

OBJECTIVES
The core objective of the project was to solve the research problem by finding answers to the above questions.

HYPOTHESIS
An existential and phenomenological engagement with place can have a transformative impact on our earlier perceptions.

DELIMITATIONS AND LIMITATIONS
There were two major delimitations to the present study:
1. The first was to keep the entire research confined to a single point of reference, that of Christian-Muslim relations in Eastleigh.
2. The second was to limit the study to seeing whether mapping made any difference in the perceptions of the mappers. Finding the causes of such differences would require another study and was therefore left out and recommended as an issue for further research.

As for limitations, there were several, and serious ones:
1. Overcoming the already underlying suspicion among members of the mapping team comprised of Christians and Muslims.
2. Assuring the community of our good intentions in mapping.
3. Coping with security-related fears in a volatile area (indeed one of the mapped streets was bombed just a day after the exercise!)

Research in Mapping

Mapping communities for appraisal of various factors is common in our times. In Chapter 1 Willem Jansen has mentioned earlier mapping projects in Eastleigh. In 2008 the present writer conducted a project in Mukuru, Nairobi for community health asset mapping.

"Mapping" is a vast term, embracing cross-discipline contexts in numerous and varied ways.[68] For our narrower purpose, we may look at mapping in three broad (sometimes overlapping) categories, namely, (1) Natural mapping, (2) Social mapping, and (3) Personal mapping.

Natural mapping is a geomorphologic enterprise resulting in generating atlas maps and is not of our direct concern. Social mapping and personal mapping fell more into our mosaic in the context of the present project. Social or community mapping is a commonly used tool in participatory community appraisals these days. When we hear of such terms as "poverty mapping", "crime mapping" or "health assets mapping" (as was done in Mukuru in 2008), or Gender Based Violence "GBV Mapping" (as was done by another organization in Eastleigh in 2012), we are talking of looking at community-spatiality, many times from an objective observational point of view. In the Mukuru project, for example, we used Geographical Informational Systems (GIS) maps to plot into them the community health assets that we had identified by our direct observation.

The Eastleigh exercise, however, was basically marked by the third (and not too common) type of mapping, namely, personal mapping. This type seems to have been inspired by a branch of geography known as "Human Geography," ushered in by the writings of John Kirtland Wright (1891-1969). The essence of J. K. Wright's argument is as follows:

1. Both map makers and map users are human. This means that "every map is a reflection partly of objective realities and partly of subjective elements. No map can be wholly objective."[69] This experience continues when one's maps are interpreted in a group by others.
2. The process of map-making and map-using involves the human process of imagination.
3. By including the aesthetic imagination in mapping, Wright has referred to the metaphorical euphemism of *Terrae Incognitae* [unknown lands].[70] Such a bold and

---

[68] An internet search for "mapping" returned 168,000,000 hits on 30 March 2013.

[69] J. K. Wright, 'Map makers are human: Comments on the subjective in maps.' *Geographical Review* 32: (1942): 527-44.

[70] Almost every map has territories marked as *Terrae Incognitae*. Toby Lester has called the entire Chapter Nine of his book 'Terrae Incognitae.' Toby Lester, *The Fourth Part of the World* (New York: Free Press, 2009), 166-179. In his epigraph to this chapter (p. 166), Lester attributes this term to Ptolemy's *Geography*. Interestingly, Wright's name is not included in Lester's massive bibliography.

creative step is apt to disturb the scientific purists who, in Wright's words, would want to leave it 'to the artists, poets, philosophers, novelists, and politicians to develop the aesthetic and intuitive faculties of their minds; [and recommend that] geographers should keep to a straighter and narrower path.'[71] Obviously Wright does not agree with this stereotyping. In the context of our project, when we walked the streets of Eastleigh, we were not only mapping the known land of the streets, we were also mapping the *Terrae Incognitae* of Christian-Muslim relationships.

Personal mapping, owing a lot of its theoretical basis to the human geographic work of Wright, seems to have shifted the scholarly focus from the category of "maps" to the category of "mapping" as a form of human behaviour, as the theoretical geographer James M. Blaut points out.[72]

Mapping behaviour and how mapping impacts the mappers has been studied mostly in relation to children, but also in relation to adults. With reference to children, it has inspired numerous studies. M. H. Mathews, for example has used it to study children's environmental cognition using Free Recall Maps (children were asked to draw maps of their home areas based on their memories).[73] In the area of religion and theology we have two remarkable studies using mapping to determine children's concepts of God.[74] We might also recall the studies by Stella Vosniadou & William F Brewer,[75] Joseph R. Boyle,[76] and Shu-Chiu LIU.[77] All these scholars in various contexts and various times have studied how mapping contributes to children's cognition of various realities.

With reference to the mapping behaviour in adults and how mapping impacts on the mappers, there have been a number of studies. Daniel Montello, for instance, writing in the context of cognitive mapping has observed, "Maps *re*-present the world by providing versions of truth

---

[71] Wright, 'Terrae Incognitae,' 7.

[72] James M. Blaut, David Stea, Christopher Spencer, and Mark Blades, 'Mapping as a Cultural and Cognitive Universal, *Annals of the Association of American Geographers*, Vol. 93, No. 1 (Mar., 2003): 165. Stable URL: http://www.jstor.org/stable/1515329. Accessed: 04/04/2009 04:04. James M. Blaut, 'Natural Mapping,' *Transactions of the Institute of British Geographers*, New Series, Vol. 16, No. 1 (1991), pp. 55. Stable URL: http://www.jstor.org/stable/622906. Accessed: 25/03/2009 03:54.

[73] M. H. Matthews, 'Cognitive Mapping Abilities of Young Boys and Girls,' *Geography*, Vol. 69, No. 4 (October 1984): 334. Stable URL: http://www.jstor.org/stable/40570882.Accessed: 24/02/2013. M. H. Matthews, 'Environmental Cognition of Young Children: Images of Journey to School and Home Area,' *Transactions of the Institute of British Geographers,* New Series, Vol. 9, No. 1 (1984): 103. Stable URL: http://www.jstor.org/stable/621869.Accessed: 24/02/2013 10:30.

[74] One is by David Kunkel and others. See Mark A. Kunkel, Stephen Cook, David S. Meshel, Donald Daughtry, and Anita Hauenstein, 'God Images: A Concept Map,' *Journal for the Scientific Study of Religion*, Vol. 38, No. 2 (Jun., 1999): 193-202. Stable URL: http://www.jstor.org/stable/1387789.Accessed: 23/07/2011 13:44. The other one is by David M. Csinos. See David M. Csinos, 'Four Ways of Knowing God: Exploring Children's Spiritual Styles,' *Journal of Childhood and Religion* Volume 1, Issue 8 (December 2010): 1-32. http://www.childhoodandreligion.com/JCR/Volume_1_(2010)_files/Csinos%20Dec%202010.pdf Accessed 1 July 2011.

[75] Stella Vosniadou and William F. Brewer, 'Mental Models of Earth: A Study of Conceptual Change in Childhood,' *Cognitive Psychology* 24 (1992): 535-585.

[76] Joseph R. Boyle, 'The Effects of a Cognitive Mapping Strategy on the Literal and Inferential Comprehension of Students with Mild Disabilities,' *Learning Disability Quarterly,* Vol. 19, No. 2 (Spring, 1996): 86-98 Stable URL: http://www.jstor.org/stable/1511250. Accessed: 16/04/2009 03:07.

[77] Shu-Chiu LIU, 'Historical Models and Science Instruction,' A Cross Cultural Analysis Based on Students' Views,' *Asia Pacific Forum on Science Learning and Teaching*, Vol 7 Issue 2 (2006).

for human minds to apprehend. In turn, minds represent the world too, internally as "cognitive maps."[78]

In another study on the 'Social Determinants of Health' in St. James Town in Canada in 2009, a process of participatory mapping approach was used. The following words coming from the conclusion of that study are of interest to our purpose:

> The Community Mapping process provided newcomer residents with a way to express the fusion of their inner and out [sic] worlds – their *sense of place,* or lack thereof, in an effort to come to a better understanding of their lived experiences.[79]

Owing to space constraints in this chapter, we might not be able to offer a thorough canvas of the theoretical frameworks of postmodern theorists of spatiality. But we might certainly recall the epoch-making names of Henri Lefebvre, who has argued that space (especially urban space) is "ideologically produced" in our times, the human geographer Yi-Fu Tuan who has talked of "topophilia" (love of place) and "topophobia" (fear of place), Edward Casey who has contributed significantly to discussing the phenomenology of place (human experience of place), Edward Relf who has talked of "placelesssness" (to describe the urban dwellers' feeling living in apartment buildings), and Edward B. Soja who has talked of the "trialectics" or "thirding" of space (involving the spatial, historical, and social dimensions of the being).

All the above seem to have a tremendous bearing on the personal approach that we used in mapping Eastleigh for Christian-Muslim relations. We could see space as "ideologically produced" in Eastleigh (Lefebvre) in the high economic interdependence between Christians and Muslims. We could feel the love and fear of the place (Yi-Fu Tuan), and so on.

Significance

Thus, using a personal, existential, phenomenological type of approach to community mapping has sought to offer an experimental catalyst. This has been done by filling the knowledge gaps in the earlier recorded literature, since no similar methodology has been used to map Christian-Muslim relations in relation to urban spatiality. The exercise has sought to create interesting new knowledge concerning Christian-Muslim relations arising out of a human engagement with the mapped spatiality.

Data Interpretation and Analysis

I have already discussed the phenomenological method we used for collecting, interpreting and analyzing data in Eastleigh in my earlier section on "Research in Mapping." Presently, I will discuss what we actually learnt about Christian-Muslim relations by mapping the streets of Eastleigh. This has been done through four perspectives, namely, space as observed reality, space as lived experience, the phenomenology of mapping, and lessons learnt for Christian-Muslim relations.

SPACE AS OBSERVED REALITY

The human cognitive engagement with space and place through mapping offers space first as an observed reality. Participants mapping the twelve streets of Section 1 of Eastleigh had

---
[78] Ibid.
[79] www.wellesleyinstitute.com/.../SJT-Initiative's-Community-Mapping-...Accessed 5 March 2013.

each been supplied with a mapping datasheet in which to record their observations about the place as they drew maps of the same. These datasheets have been analysed and collated into four matrices at the end of this chapter. A further analysis of these matrices indicates the following:

The Contrasting Diversity

Maps of the twelve streets revealed a contrasting diversity in terms of the physical space. There appeared to be a general (though not necessarily uniformed) upward movement from Street 1 to Street 12. In other words, Street 1 could be placed somewhere towards the lowest on the scale of physical appearance in terms of cleanliness, infrastructure, economy, and security. On the other hand, Street 12 could be placed somewhere towards the highest on this scale.

Human experience of space as observed reality would derive from the three basic sensory routes: visual, auditory, and olfactory. The Eastleigh mapppers also used the same sensory routes of observation and found that the twelve streets offered contrasting pictures via almost every sensory route. Below is an observational inventory of the 12 streets that we mapped.

A Streetwise Observational Inventory

Visual

- Slums at the end (Street 1)
- Sloppy and slimy (Street 1)
- Poor drainage system (Street 1)
- Tall buildings, schools (Street 1)

- Fair drainage system (Street 2)
- Sloppy area (Street 2)
- Careless disposal of plastic waste (Street 2)
- Filthy and muddy (Street 2)

- Population well distributed (Street 3)
- Place with slum lifestyle (Street 3)

- Road in bad shape (Street 4)
- Both residential and commercial houses (Street 4)

- Old buildings (Street 6)

- Dark (Street 7)
- Overcrowded with businesses and also idlers and beggars (Street 7)
- Many hotels and an inn (Street 7)
- Permanent houses (Street 7)
- Poor refurbished buildings (Street 7)
- Largely occupied with Somali refugees (Street 7)

- Old buildings (Street 9)

- Permanent buildings towards the end (Street 10)

- Buildings from the First Avenue are temporary (Street 10)
- Different businesses (Street 10)
- Untidy and disorganized (Street 10)
- Attractive billboard (Street 10

- Very busy street (Street 11)
- Not clean (Street 11)
- Poor waste disposal (Street 11)

- Very big shopping malls (Street 12)
- Many banks (Street 12)
- Many hotels (Street 12)
- Booking offices for buses (Street 12)
- Safest street in Eastleigh (Street 12)

Auditory

- Fairly peaceful (Street 3)
- Upper part busy and noisy while lower part quiet (Street 4)
- Noisy (Street 6 and 7)
- Noisy (Street 9)
- A bit quiet since no loud music compared to other streets (Street 8)

Olfactory

- The place smells (Street 1)
- Foul smell (Street 2)
- Not much smell (Street 3)
- Mixed smells of meat roasting and petrol fumes (Street 4)
- Upper part smelly (Street 5)
- Smelly (Street 6)
- Foul smell because of improper garbage disposal and poor drainage system (Street 7)
- Stinky (Street 7)
- Stinking (Street 9)
- Mixed odors of sewage and the sweet aroma of Somali food (Street 10)

The contrasting diversity characterizing physical space in the 12 mapped streets in Section A seems to become evident from the above inventory. Since our interest was not purely cognitive, a detailed analysis and interpretation would fall outside our immediate interest. But one thing for our purpose became clear after mapping: that Street 12 is apparently the most affluent, the cleanest, and the safest.

A Community Asset Inventory
Asset mapping is a line by itself in participatory community appraisals. Although community asset mapping was not our primary goal, we did try to map out the most visible community assets on the 12 streets of Section A, since community asset mapping helps us to prepare community asset inventories and thus may help us understand the issues related to space-contest, justice, and Christian-Muslim relations.

The following is a streetwise community asset inventory of Section A in Eastleigh.

Street 1

None reported

Street 2

- Several *Madrasas (Muslim religious schools)*
- A Children's Home
- Some institutions have only one religion
- Others have both Christians and Muslims
- Churches: PCEA, Full Gospel, Revival Centre
- Several Language centres
- VCT (Voluntary Testing and Counseling for HIV and AIDS)
- Mama Fatuma Children's Home

Street 3

- Kiosks
- Mosque
- *Madarasa*
- Private and Public schools
- Churches: PCEA, Deliverance Church
- Islamic College
- Shops
- Garage

Street 4

- M-Pesa services[80] and public telephones available
- Maina Wanjige Secondary School
- Mosques
- *Madarasa*
- Muslim Medical Clinic
- County Council Medical Clinic

Street 5

- Medical facilities mostly owned by Muslims
- Pharmacy run by Christian-Muslim business partnership
- Faith-Based institutions help all equally
- Christian Industrial Training Institute (CITI)
- Businesses are owned by Christian-Muslim partnership

Street 6

- Public phone shops and international phone services available
- Abdullahi Abu Abbas Madarasa
- Al-Ansar Nursery and Primary School

---

[80] M-Pesa service is a money transfer service via mobile phones, widely available in Kenya

- A mosque
- Islamic Bookshop
- Islamic dress shop
- Businesses (saloon, beauty, bureau, banks)

Street 7

- Mosques
- Banks

Street 8

- One mosque and two churches
- Centre for Christian Muslim Relations
- Many shops (boutiques, fast food, money exchange)
- Hotels and lodgings

Street 9

- Islamic Bookshop
- Ibnu Abbas School of Qur'anic Studies
- Kenya Muslim Charitable Society
- Volunteer Youth Services
- Rafiki Clinic
- No churches

Street 10

- Every lodging has its "mosque"
- No churches

Street 11

- No mosques or churches
- A Somali-owned Chemist shop is operated by Christians
- Financial stability
- Shops well stocked

Street 12

- Very big shopping malls
- Many banks
- Many hotels
- Booking offices for buses
- Mosques
- Eastleigh High School
- Banks, supermarkets, hotels and other businesses
- No churches, only mosques

From the above it may be noted that Street 1 is the poorest in terms of community assets while Street 12 is the richest. Churches are only on Streets 2 and 3. Mosques are on Streets 3, 4, 6, 7, 8, and 10. Streets 1, 5, 9, and 11 have neither any church nor any mosque.

SPACE AS LIVED EXPERIENCE

The previous section "Space as Observed Reality" does not merely help to see space as a detached object "out there." That "detached" type of approach to space might characterize Geographical Informational Systems (GIS) mapping. In our phenomenological type of approach to mapping, we might note that the sensory observational characteristics of space in terms of its sights, sounds and smells all emerge as a result of human experience of space. Such characteristics may help to see space as part of us and us as part of space.

During the present exercise we attempted to map the twelve streets of Eastleigh along three major variables to understand Eastleigh space as a lived experience. These variables were: Space contest in relation to space distribution, Christian-Muslim harmony or Conflict in relation to space, and Justice.

Space Contest in Relation to Space Distribution
Space distribution in relation to Christian-Muslim occupancy appeared marked by the same uneven and contrasting broad-strokes as the observed appearance of physical space. Some mapping teams felt that space was "equally" or evenly distributed among Christians and Muslims (Streets 1, 2, 3, 5, 10, 11, and 12). Some mapppers found such distribution to be uneven or "random" (Streets 2 and 5). Others observed that space distribution was skewed in favour of Muslims in such a manner that Muslims occupied economically prime spaces where Christians were concentrated in slum type areas (Streets 3, 4, 6, 7, 8, 9, and 12). The overlap here seems interesting. Streets 1, 2, and 5 are described as having both "equal" and "random" distribution. On the other hand Streets 3 and 12 have been described as both "equal" and skewed in favour of Muslim occupancy. This indicates that one cannot talk of "Muslim Streets" or "Christian Streets" in Eastleigh. This means that all streets are dotted almost equally with Christian-Muslim neighborhoods. Such a finding can have a significant bearing on understanding Christian-Muslim relations in Eastleigh.

In terms of space contest, Streets 1, 2, 5, 10, and 11 were described as having no space contest while the rest of the streets were described as "overcrowded" to the extent of encroaching road reserves. Somali Muslims dominated the economically prime space. But, interestingly, on all streets, the mappers were quick to point out that space contest did not result in any Christian-Muslim conflicts. On the other hand, Christians and Muslims seemed to have devised their own creative and mutually-rewarding ways to share among themselves the fruits of the economy of space. This was seen mainly at two levels: (1) Christians and Muslims employing one another in their businesses (although some mappers felt that such employment opportunities were not equally shared among the two faiths in that Christians tended to get lower jobs in Muslim-owned businesses and workplaces). (2) Christians and Muslims owned and operated businesses together in joint partnerships.

Christian-Muslim Harmony or Conflict in Relation to Space
Mappers on almost every street described Christian-Muslim relations as "harmonious," "fairly good," "very good," "Excellent," and even "in love!" However, on Streets 2, 3, 4, 5, 6, and 7, such relations were found marked with mutual fears and suspicions. Only one mapper

described the relation as "not in harmony" (Street 6). Interestingly, Street 6 also belongs to the first group of streets describing Christian-Muslim relations as "harmonious". This only seems to underscore our recurrent finding that space as lived experience transcends the neat, detached "cut-and dried" type of pure objectivism often featuring in the gadget-generated GIS mapping.

As for Christian-Muslim conflict in relation to space, once again, the reports were contrasting and overlapping. On the one hand some groups of mappers reported no conflict and that Christians and Muslims were living in harmony (Streets 1, 2, 5, 9, 10, 11, and 12). On the other hand other groups reported occasional conflicts (Streets 2, 3, 4, 5, 6, 7, and 8). Such conflicts were caused by the following variables: (1) General mistrust of one another, (2) Christian converts fearing reprisals by Muslims, (3) Too much space-contest at times (like in one case space contest over the use of a toilet!), (4) Mistaken identities (associating all Muslims either with the Somalis or with terrorists), and (5) Cultural differences. Interestingly, in this case, except Street 2, the remaining streets seem more neatly distributed in terms of conflict zones than has been the case with other variables. This might call for further research and investigation as to the causes of such zoning, or even to re-verify the mappers' earlier impressions about such zoning.

Justice
Finally, space as "lived experience" would involve the issue of justice. Mappers looked at the issues of justice along the variables of religious, social, economic, and gender. Freedom of worship was reported on Streets 1 and 8 (which does not mean such freedom is not available on other streets merely because it was not reported!). Other mappers reported a general environment of religious, social, economic and gender justice (Streets 2, 5, 7, 11, and 12). On the other hand Streets 3, 6, 8, and 10 were found to be marked with cases of injustice. Mostly there was talk of economic injustice in that Christians felt deprived of equal economic opportunities, job cadres, and wage scales in Muslim-owned businesses. Once again, the zoning off of streets in terms of socio-economic justice is noteworthy.

When it comes to gender-justice, there were mixed reports. Streets 2, 8, 11, and 12 were reported to have gender-justice in that women were free to participate in economy (Street 8); women-men ratio was 3:1 in Atlas College enrollment (Street 8); women worked in front desk jobs (Street 8); And men and women related well and equally participated in socio-economic activities (Street 11 and 12). On the other hand, Streets 2, 6, and 9 were found to have cases of gender-injustice in which women felt dominated by men and were not given equal opportunities.

Based on the above section on "Space as lived experience" the following street matrix may be drawn.

A Street Matrix in Terms of Conflict Zones

Conflict Variable	Street Number
Christian-Muslim Conflict in relation to space	2, 3, 4, 5, 6, 7, and 8
Christian Muslim Conflict in relation to justice	3, 6, 8, and 10
Gender Conflict in relation to justice	2, 6, and 9
Streets mentioned more than once	2, 3, and 6

The above might call for re-mapping Streets 2, 3, and 9 to better understand the conflict variables and how conflicts can be resolved. On the other hand the apparently statistical character of the above approach might not prove to be entirely reliable for concluding about existential issues on these streets. Indeed the grenade attack that occurred just a day after concluding the mapping exercise took place on Street 2.

THE PHENOMENOLOGY OF MAPPING

The third analytical route of mapping data is phenomenological, by which we mean taking human experience into scientific cognizance while studying space. In our particular case, the human experience that we took cognizance of was that of the mappers. The phenomenological approach to mapping recognizes the fact that maps are not merely products of detached observations of places or "objective" interviews of people occupying those places. Maps may actually signify the human engagement with place and the resultant human transformation. Such an experience could be comparable to Jacob's "Aha" experience at Bethel when he exclaimed "Surely God was in this place and I knew it not!."

For our purpose, we studied whether the experience of mapping helped transform the mappers' perceptions, and if so, in what way. Such perception was studied under two broad categories: the mappers' perception of mapping itself and their perception of Christian-Muslim relations. Both these variables were studied on a before-after basis.

Phenomenology of Mapping-I

(Mapppers' Perception of Mapping Before-After)

NB: The "Before-After" cross responses are from the same respondent

Before Mapping	After Mapping
1. I thought it was a means of counting buildings and making maps	Mapping is a vital process for understanding people in relation to place
2. We started at the end of the street looking at buildings and infrastructures	We learnt about buildings and infrastructures.
3. I felt insecure and nervous because of the terrorist activities in Eastleigh area	I learnt a lot and gained new knowledge
4. I had no idea what the project was	I visited many religious places for both

	all about	Christians and Muslims and learnt how they share life together. That was wonderful. I like it! I now understand what mapping is.
5.	I had a negative perception of mapping. Thought it could generate suspicion.	My perception changed and became positive. People welcomed us and gave us all the information we needed.
6.	I thought it was a complicated exercise and of no benefit	It is a worthwhile exercise because it has empowered me.
7.	I did not think it was going to be interesting or I would learn anything from it. I didn't think that this exercise would help in improving Christian-Muslim relations	I realized how important the exercise was as it helped to strengthen Christian-Muslim relations.
8.	I was confused. I perceived it to be very difficult, especially in a Muslim dominated area.	After the exercise my confusion went away. The exercise was enjoyable and added to my knowledge.
9.	I could not imagine I would be asked to engage in such an exercise. I thought mapping has no meaning or impact on me.	After mapping I became more familiar with my place and community than I was before.
10.	I was fearing to be harassed because Christians and Muslims were not in good relationship	I am positively changed about my views on Muslims. [I have come to realize that] they do respect Christians.
11.	I thought it was going to be a complicated and boring activity. I did not understand its scope.	Mapping is really an enjoyable thing since it helps one to understand his surrounding that he thought he understood.
12.	I though mapping meant [just] looking at buildings and representing them on paper.	After the mapping [I learnt to] interact with the place and found issues about religious, social, and psychological relations [of people] in relation to place.
13.	I thought mapping meant looking at buildings, roads, electricity, and [means of] communication.	It gave me an opportunity of sharing [in] social relationships like schools, mosques, and churches.
14.	I thought I would interact with people in this area and write down the names of the buildings	[After mapping] I realized how people interact with space and place, infrastructure and issues of justice
15.	I though mapping meant identifying places [especially] religious institutions	It is a very enjoyable exercise. Becomes threatening at times when people do not agree with your findings. [in sum] mapping is enjoyable and adventurous.
16.	I was afraid of the insecurity. I thought it was a Muslim dominated area. I had never learnt mapping before, so it would be a hard task.	Mapping is not a 'solid' but 'liquid' process. Muslims in Eastleigh are not the cause of insecurity. They are welcoming people.
17.	I thought mapping involved identifying the physical aspects in a geographical location	Mapping is not about the structures and geographical land map. It helps to understand people and their relationships.
18.	I was wondering why Christians [from St. Paul's] wanted to map Muslims in Eastleigh	I realized that Eastleigh is one of the best places to do mapping because of its diversity
19.	I thought mapping was about the place and not about people	[Mapping helped me to] define place in relation to people, especially security, economy, and ethnicity aspects.

20. I had never done mapping and was never interested in it	Even though I lived in Eastleigh, I did not [know] anything in my environment. But [after mapping] now I know. I am absolutely happy. It was a wonderful experience. I wish I could join university for mapping
21. I thought it would be very difficult and it would have to do with measuring roads and buildings	I realized that mapping [helped me to] understand myself, the place, and the community [better].
22. I had no interest in it and did not think it was important anyway.	It was very interesting, exciting and fact-finding. Now I know Eastleigh better than I had ever known it.
23. I thought Muslims would not cooperate with mapping	Muslims are good people to work with. They are friendly.
24. It was my second time mapping.	I learnt a lot and understood people better

From the above table it becomes evident that before mapping the majority of the participants had two common perceptions: (a) that mapping would involve mere observation of buildings, and (b) that mapping was a rather curious and somewhat unsafe activity to study Christian-Muslim relations.

After the mapping, the participants' two perceptions of mapping both changed in almost the opposite direction. The following codes can illustrate this new shift.

Mapping helps to understand place in relation to people
1. Mapping is a vital process for understanding people in relation to place (1).
2. After mapping I became more familiar with my place and community than I was before (9).
3. Mapping is really an enjoyable thing since it helps one to understand his surrounding that he thought he understood (11).
4. [After mapping] I realized how people interact with space and place, infrastructure and issues of justice (14).
5. Mapping is not about the structures and geographical land map. It helps to understand people and their relationships (17).
6. [Mapping helped me to] define place in relation to people, especially security, economy, and ethnicity aspects (19).
7. I realized that mapping [helped me to] understand myself, the place, and the community [better] (21).

Mapping helped to understand Christian-Muslim relations better
1. I visited many religious places for both Christians and Muslims and learnt how they share life together. That was wonderful. I like it! I now understand what mapping is (4).
2. I realized how important the exercise was as it helped to strengthen Christian-Muslim relations (7).
3. I am positively changed about my views on Muslims. [I have come to realize that] they do respect Christians (10).
4. Mapping is not a 'solid' but 'liquid' process. Muslims in Eastleigh are not the cause of insecurity. They are welcoming people (16).

The second variable was the change in the mappers' perception of Christian-Muslim relations after mapping. Once again, the change in perception was drastic as indicated from the following Table.

Phenomenology of Mapping-II

(Mappers' Perception of Christian-Muslim Relations Before-After)

NB: The "Before-After" cross responses are from the same respondent

	Before Mapping	**After Mapping**
1.	*[Christian]* I thought Christians and Muslims cannot relate because Eastleigh is a Muslim dominated area where Christians were not allowed to live.	I realized that there is mutual coexistence between Christians and Muslims. Living together they exchange a lot together to the extent that some Christians offer worship services to both Muslims and Christians.
2.	*[Muslim]* We thought Christians and Muslims were [in] rivalry	After [mapping] we learnt that they were peaceful. Christians and Muslims were living in harmony. Everybody has freedom of worship.
3.	*[Christian]* In Early October when St. Polycarp Church was attacked, I thought that Christians were attacked by Muslims. That made me suspicious and nervous at first.	There is harmonious coexistence between Christians and Muslims. There is no clear borderline between them. Only at prayers do they separate.
4.	*[Muslim]* I thought they hate one another because of their differences.	Now I learnt that how close Christian and Muslims are! Their children play and eat together. And I like it!
5.	*[Christian]* My perception of Christian Muslim relations was quite negative because I thought that there were faith based and economic issues [between the two faiths]	My perception [after mapping] became positive. Both Christians and Muslims live together in harmony sharing businesses, jobs, and other challenges of life.
6.	*[Christian]* I thought that Christians and Muslims have no parallel lines and they are in bad relationship.	They [Christians and Muslims] are cordially living together in harmony.
7.	*[Muslim]* My perception [before mapping] was that relationship between Muslims and Christians was bad and they could not work together.	After the [mapping] exercise I realized that the relation between Muslims and Christians is good and they both depend on each other.
8.	*[Christian]* I had the concept that Christians and Muslims could not work together, especially in the area of religious understanding. I was scared on the first day thinking that Muslims might attack us....I did not believe they could work amicably with us.	Now I know that an effort towards Muslims can result in something good. As the days [of mapping exercise] went by, [my] suspicion went away, or reduced drastically. I was much more surprised when I was told that a certain pharmacy is co-owned by a Christian and a Muslim who are good friends. Now I am convinced that Christians and Muslims can do many things together.
9.	*[Muslim]* I believed that Christians and Muslims antagonize and hate	After engaging in the mapping exercise, I came to realize that Christian Muslim relations is

	one another because of their ideological differences.	cordial. [Even though] their faith is different, they conduct business together, live together, and even intermarry.
10.	*[Christian]* My perception was that Muslims hated Christians who were the target of the Muslim *Jihads*.	Muslims respect the People of the Book (Bible readers) who are genuine and sincere. Also Christians admire Muslims, especially [for their seriousness about] prayer and fasting.
11.	*[Muslim]* My perception was that Christians-Muslim relations were not good enough for them to work together.	[I] realized that Muslim Christian relation was not bad as I [had] thought, although some Christians think that the dominant Muslims [in Eastleigh] are mistreating them. Yet majority remains in harmony and in good relations.
12.	*[Christian]* I thought that Christians and Muslims cannot coexist and can never share a common platform.	After the [mapping] exercise it [became] evident that there is co-existence between Muslims and Christians. They share lot like the infrastructure, space, and the environment.
13.	*[Muslim]* I thought Christian-Muslim relationship is very good and they live in harmony.	Christian-Muslim relationship is very good and harmonious.
14.	*[Muslim]* I thought that Muslims and Christians in this area are not totally interacting.	Muslims and Christians are friendly and interacting without any problem. They can even share opportunities equally without ethnicity.
15.	*[Christian]* I have always thought that there is a strife between Christians and Muslims though did not know the [precise] areas of strife. I also thought that it is the Muslims who have a negative attitude towards Christians.	My perception after the exercise confirmed my earlier view that there is strife between Christians and Muslims. However [after the mapping exercise] I also realize that the strife is based more on perceptions on both sides than on facts. Christians and Muslims need to realize that they both belong to the Abrahamic monotheistic faith and learn more about one another.
16.	*[Christian]* The way Christians and Muslims engage in war every time [like] Al Shabab, I believe that there is no connectedness between two people.	Christians and Muslims have a unique relationship, especially those living in Eastleigh. They work and interact together.
17.	*[Muslim]* Christians and Muslims relate with fears among themselves	Christian-Muslim relationship is not in bad state.
18.	*[Muslim]* I live in Eastleigh and know that Christians and Muslims generally live in harmony, except only a few times when there may be tension.	It was just the way I had thought before mapping.
19.	*[Christian]* I perceived Christian-Muslim relations to be arrogant.	Muslim-Christian relation is fantastic in Eastleigh. They live in harmony.
20.	*[Muslim]* I am a Somali. When I was in Somalia I never saw someone who is a Christian. I have a Christian friend, but we never discussed Muslim-Christian issues.	Muslims and Christians in Eastleigh live in even greater harmony than I had thought [before mapping].
21.	*[Christian]* I thought Muslims and Christians are not friends and can never work together. I thought Eastleigh is a Muslim place [with	☐ I came to realize that Christians and Muslims are friends. And both are people. ☐ I also realized that Christians and

	no place for Christians]	Muslims can work together in the same place. ☐ Both Christians and Muslims hire one another in the workplace and there is economic interdependence between them.
22.	*[Muslim]* I thought that Muslims relate with one another but Christians work on their own because of the religious differences and discriminations between the two.	I came to understand that there is interdependence between the two religions and they live in harmony where they are able to employ one another and work together.
23.	*[Christian]* I thought Christians and Muslims cannot work together.	Christians and Muslims can work together.
24.	*[Christian]* I thought Muslims were very harsh and discriminative.	I learnt that Christians and Muslims live and work together in harmony with each other. They employ one another in their business. They have synergistic relations.

The above Table indicates that both Christian and Muslim mappers had a clearly negative perception of Christian-Muslim relations before mapping, which changed into clearly positive after mapping.

LESSONS LEARNT FOR CHRISTIAN-MUSLIM RELATIONS
Fourthly, and finally, we deconstructed the mapping data to see what lessons it offered for Christian-Muslim relations. Mapping of Eastleigh has shed light on two hitherto unrealized variables pertaining to Christian-Muslim relations, namely economic interdependence and the ethnic factor.

Economic Interdependence
Mapping has taught us that the variable equally tying up persons and space is economy. Eastleigh is a place of high economic activity. Such activity is not divided along religious lines. Christians and Muslims interact along economic lines in two major ways:
1. Mutual employment of Christians and Muslims in the workplace
2. Business partnerships and joint ownerships of businesses by Christians and Muslims in Eastleigh

The Ethnic Factor
Another significant variable is the ethnic factor. Before mapping, the common perception (at least on the part of the SPU team) was that Eastleigh was a homogeneously Somali-Muslim place. After mapping, two things became clear: (a) Eastleigh also has a Christian population, and (b) Muslims are not homogenously Somalis. There are also Muslims of other ethnic origins (like the Borana, for example) in Eastleigh, and the ethnic competition plays up between communities in Eastleigh without much necessary mitigation from a common faith.

Conclusion

SUMMARY OF FINDINGS

The mapping exercise in Eastleigh helped us to find the following:

1. There is a contrasting diversity in the twelve mapped streets in terms of "space as observed reality".
2. A community asset inventory indicates that assets are more located in Streets 6-12 than on Streets 1-5 (although this may not be always uniform).
3. Street 12 was found to be the most economically active and safest street.
4. Streets 2, 3, and 6 were identified as "Conflict Zones" (wording mine).
5. Although there were contrasting reports as regards justice and economic interdependence, generally there was justice and high economic interdependence.
6. Mapping, by way of an existential engagement with spatiality, radically transformed the mappers' perceptions. 23 out of 24 of the members of the teams, regardless of their faith, were surprised to see how their perception of Christian-Muslim relations changed from negative to positive after mapping Eastleigh. Mapper 18 did not see any change in his perception since he always believed that Christians and Muslims always live in harmony in Eastleigh anyway.

RECOMMENDATIONS

Based on the findings of the above study, the following recommendations may be made:

1. There is an urgent need to mitigate the environmental hazards caused by poor waste management. Now that it was established that Christians and Muslims existed by and large in harmony and good relations, joint cleaning ventures could be undertaken by Christians and Muslims in Eastleigh.
2. Many Muslim students from Eastleigh expressed the desire to be invited to St. Paul's University for more engagements and joint opportunities. This is something worth looking into.
3. Having learnt of the good news of the general harmony, good neighborliness and economic interdependence between Christians and Muslims in Eastleigh, there is now need for people of the two faiths to come together and carry joint programmes for fostering Christian-Muslim relations.
4. Similar mapping exercises could be carried out in other parts of Eastleigh and findings compared.

ISSUES FOR FURTHER RESEARCH

1. Deeper and more systematic research into Christian-Muslim relations in relation to a phenomenological study of spatiality.
2. More comparative studies along similar lines in other spatialities to valididate our findings.
3. Comparative studies in Christian-Muslim relations in relation to spatiality in West Africa, the Middle East, India and other parts of the world.
4. A scientific reexamination of phenomenological data obtained from the present research.
5. Further research employing ex post facto design to determine the causes of our findings

CHAPTER SEVEN

How Mapping Can Build Christian-Muslim Relationships

The Story of Susan Olulo and Kaltuma Mohammed

Willem Jansen

During several intensive days in Eastleigh, Susan and Kaltuma form a casual pair, but may end up becoming lifetime friends. They have met for a "mapping" project organized by the Centre for Christian-Muslim Relations in Eastleigh (CCMRE). The "mapping team" of Susan and Kaltuma, which started by finding out each other's origin and religion, gradually develops into a cautious friendship.

Susan Olulu is a theology student at St. Paul's University in Limuru, Kenya. In her hometown of Kisumu in West-Kenya, she is an active member of *God's Last Appeal Church*, an independent African church. Kaltuma Mohammed is a student of Nutrition Sciences at a Technical College in Nairobi. In Moyale, her hometown on the border of Kenya and Ethiopia, Kaltuma often used to go to the mosque. Now that she lives in Eastleigh, she attends prayers less frequently. She belongs to the Borana tribe, one of the 41 tribes of Kenya. Both Kaltuma and Susan live about 700 kilometres away from their homes and they now meet in this intriguing place of Eastleigh.

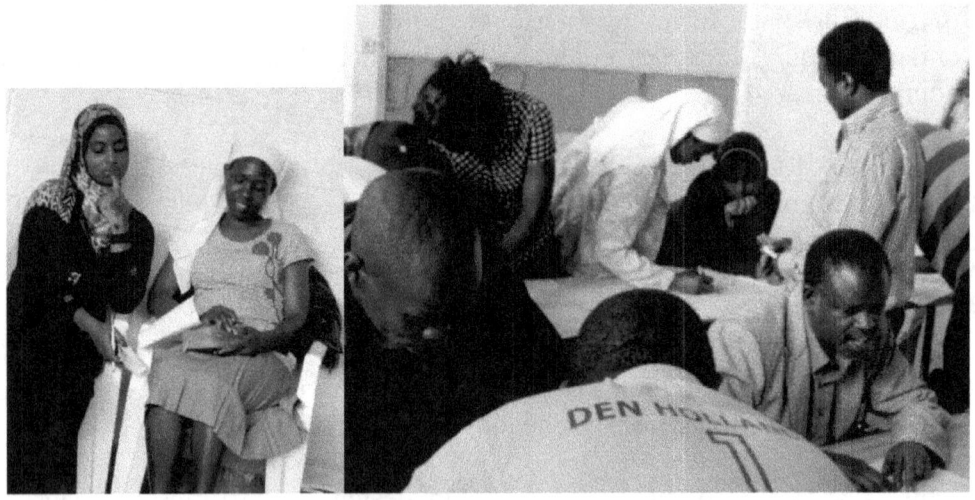

[Photo Left: Newfound Friends: Kaltuma (in Black) and Susan (in White Headscarf). Photo Right: "A Friend in Mapping is a Friend Indeed": Susan and Kaltuma Join in Constructing a Map of Their Street][81]

---

[81] All photo credits in this chapter and the 'mapping pictorial' belong to Willem Jansen.

'Little Mogadishu'

Eastleigh is a place bustling with people like Susan and Kaltuma. No one knows the exact number of people that live there: estimates range from 70,000 up to 300,000. Many inhabitants, especially Somalis, look upon Eastleigh as a kind of transit to more prosperous destinations. This is the district where the well-known Somali-Dutch politician, Ayaan Hirsi Ali, together with her family settled down in Eastleigh, before she left for The Hague (from where she re-emigrated to the US). Just like Ali, many others are hoping for a better future somewhere else in the world. Presently, the destination for many Somali immigrants might be Mogadishu once again, since after more than 20 years of civil war, Somalia has begun to regain at least some semblance of peace and order.

Eastleigh is known as "Little Mogadishu", because of its large numbers of Somali traders and travellers. Dotted by its shopping malls, Eastleigh today constitutes one of the largest business hubs of East Africa. Due to its activities and continuous (international and urban) migration, no other district of Nairobi is quite as multicultural as Eastleigh. Here you will come across people from almost all parts of Africa and Asia. Many Kenyans and non-Kenyans alike, however, tend to avoid Eastleigh as a *no-go area*. To many people the district is known as an area where pirate booty is laundered and illegally traded, a place where Somalis buy the scarcely-available goods from the Kenyans and where great danger looms from the *al-Qaida*-linked, terrorist group *al-Shabaab*. 'The tail of this group is in Somalia', as a Kenyan politician put it recently, 'but its head is in Eastleigh'. Now that *al-Shabaab* may have lost the war in Somalia, this terrorist group appears to threaten Eastleigh more frequently.

Eastleigh on the Map

On Eighth Street, Eastleigh, the Centre of Christian-Muslim Relations was established in 2010 under the umbrella of St. Paul's University. This is the place where Susan and Kaltuma meet for the first time in November 2012 for the mapping project, in which over 30 Muslim and Christian students and staff are participating. For three continuous days, they work two by two, as religiously mixed pairs, to map the streets of Eastleigh. Eastleigh is a religious town. Every street houses an abundance of religious buildings, as Kaltuma and Susan find out during the mapping project.

Susan and Kaltuma are to be concerned with Eighth Street. The remaining eleven streets are to be dealt with by the other 'mixed pairs'. The workshop leader, Peter, asks students to pay careful attention to everything to be mapped by them: What is striking about Eighth Street? According to Susan and Kaltuma it is the *Obama-Shop*, which is named after the most well-known person of Luo-Kenyan descent in the world. There will also be questions like *How about safety?* And *what do you learn about Muslim-Christian relationships in this street?*

[Photo Left: Susan Watches Mappers at Work. Photo Right: A Map of One of the Streets]

Tempers Start Flaring Up: The Hot Spots on the Maps

Susan and Kaltuma enter a shopping centre on 'their' street. By interviewing people they discover that here both Christians and Boranas are discriminated against by the Somalis. When they later report this conclusion to the plenary, the observation does not go over well with their fellow students. *How can these girls talk like this?* Tempers start flaring up. During the break a discussion between them and Susan raises emotions. For a moment, we begin to fear that the project is going to collapse because of inter-ethnic mistrust, which others may misconstrue to mean Christian-Muslim hostility. Kaltuma does not give her opinion directly, but agrees with Susan: Christians and Muslims discriminate against one another, but so do Muslims amongst themselves on ethnic grounds.

[Photo: "A Time to Discuss": A Group of Mappers, With Susan in the Foreground, Willem in the Mid-ground, and Kaltuma Seated Extreme Right]

Fortunately, the next day everybody is present again. The mapping specialist from India, C. B. Peter, refers to yesterday's tensions based on his expert knowledge: not all inhabitants of Eastleigh are Somali Muslims, neither are all students at St. Paul's Christians. In their turn, not all Boranas are Muslims either. Even the Vice-Chancellor of St. Paul's University is a Borana Christian. The actual Muslim or the actual Christian exists only in theory. In reality, however, they both are conditioned each by their own spatiality. This new perspective helps to reassure Susan and Kaltuma to continue their practical work. On their map, the street is shown with pictures of its mosques, *madrassahs* (Koran recitation schools), and of course the Eastleigh Fellowship Centre, which houses the Centre for Christian-Muslim Relations (CCMRE). Additionally, Kaltuma and Susan make mention of the stench from the open sewage and of the many potholes in the road. The Kenyan authorities seem not to be concerned with the infrastructure of Eastleigh.

Imam Ashafa and Pastor James

The mapping project turns out to be successful. After three days of hard work, Kaltuma and Susan hand certificates to each other. The certificates declare that in addition to theory, analysis and designing maps, they have gained practical experience in establishing Christian-Muslim relationships. For people who want to continue with this interreligious bridging, there is already an opportunity the next day. Two internationally-known guests from Nigeria, Imam Ashafa and Pastor James, are honouring the Centre for Christian-Muslim Relations with a visit. Susan and Kaltuma are both present. Pastor James tells them how he lost his hand in his fight against the Muslims in Kaduna and Jos, Nigeria, and how later he continued with the Imam on the path of peace.

[Photo: Imam Ashafa (in white) and Pastor James (in grey) visiting the CCMRE. On the far left Dr. Hassan Kinyua representing SUPKEM]

As the impressive visit to the CCMRE draws to a close with a walk around the district and a meal with camel meat, a call comes from a student of St. Paul's: *"You must come at once, a bomb has exploded"*. A hundred meters from where the students are waiting, at the other end of Eastleigh, somebody has thrown a grenade into an overcrowded *matatu* (public minibus). At least 10 people are killed, and many wounded. Almost everyone assumes that *al-Shabaab* must be behind it. This is how a meaningful day comes to a bizarre ending. Everybody in the group safely returns home, shocked by the tragedy.

[Photo: "And Here's Your Certificate": Susan Receives a "Mapper's Certificate" from Kaltuma]

United in Grief

During the next few days Kaltuma and Susan were to participate in a *Training of Trainers* elsewhere in Nairobi. But the training conducted by the Imam and the Pastor from Nigeria will not continue for Kaltuma. She receives a text message that her live-in cousin Ibrahim has died in the grenade attack. Kaltuma was the last person who had spoken to him before he got into the particular *matatu*. Various people offer to take Kaltuma home in a taxi. Kaltuma chooses Susan to accompany her to her family. After Imam Ashafa has spoken a few consoling words to Kaltuma, the mapping pair returns to Eastleigh, where Susan and Kaltuma find a family in grief. Ibrahim's parents are already on their way to Moyale, Kaltuma's hometown, to make preparations for the funeral.

[Photo: "United in Grief": Imam Ashafa consoles Kaltuma before she leaves with Susan]

On the last training day, the group of Muslims and Christians draw up a press statement to be brought along with them on their visit to Eastleigh and the families affected by the grenade attack. After weighing the pros and cons in view of safety, Susan decides to come along. In Eastleigh everything is always somehow different from what you expect. Together with the Pastor and the Imam, police and army personnel, politicians and NGO-workers, the group is forming a true peace caravan. *"No more violence. Kenya is too beautiful for that"*, sounds from a big sound truck, and *"The evildoer is poverty"*. Because of the turn of events, in the end there will be no visit of the whole group to Kaltuma's family.

[Photo: As a member of the Peace Caravan, Susan visits the spot where the matatu exploded]

During the last few days, Susan has become friends with a Muslim, despite her hesitation at this prospect at the beginning. Today she has learnt to know and "love her neighbour as herself". *"Know your neighbour!"* someone calls from a caravan. *"That's it"*, she says: *"Know your neighbour"*. On the bus, she also gets to know a sūfī-mystic, Mr. Merabaqsh Abdulaziz Bunni, a wise man who has lived in Eastleigh all his life. He is mourning too about Eastleigh, which no longer seems to display the peace of the good old days. Yet this day of the peace-caravan seems to give him – even if only for a little while – at least some hope and courage.

[Photo: "How Can We Improve Christian-Muslim Relations?" Susan with sūfī sheikh Merabaqsh Bunni]

APPENDIX 1

The Eastleigh Mapping Pictorial

Willem Jansen and C. B. Peter

It is said that a picture is worth a thousand words. The pictures below are meant to present the human face of mapping—how Christians and Muslims were brought together in renewed self-perceptions and closer bonding as a result of their existential engagamenet with place by mapping the steets of Eastleigh. [Photos: Willem Jansen]

1. Christian-Muslim Bonding through Mapping

The experience of mapping the Eastleigh spatiality afforded Christian and Muslim mappers the opportuniy to work together in mapping teams which helped them obtain social and spiritual bonding by knowing one another better than they had before.

1.1.*Where did you leave your cane?:* The cane-holding Eastleigh residents good-heartedly accept the caneless Willem Jansen in their company as they all relax outside a shop in the sprawling business centre of Eastleigh

1.2. *How many kinds of baptisms: Sprinkling, Pouring, or Immersion?* Christian and Muslim mappers mix freely as they relax by the baptismal font at the Christian-Muslim Relations Centre, Eastleigh after a grueling mapping session. Note the Islamic style of architecture and design of the baptismal font

1.3. *Smiles on both sides of the veil:* Grace and Zeituna, Eastleigh Mappers

1.4. *Bonding beyond gender:* Joan awards a certificate to her mapping teammate Tari

1.5. *Wow, victory at last!:* Muslim mappers show off their certificates at the end of the exercise as they pose with their mapping-mentor, Sheikh C. B. Peter

2. The Mapping Workshops

Eastleigh mapping was carried out systematically. First there was a training workshop where mappers were given on-the-job orientation and training into the various theoretical nuances of mapping and practical skills necessary for mappers. After thus equipped in mapping skills in the workshop, the mappers went out to "map" the streets. Then they returned to base and constructed their maps. Finally they presented their maps in an evaluation workshop. The mapping specialist from St. Paul's University, Rev. C. B. Peter facilitated these workshops

2.1. *No, this is what I actually meant by my comment at the workshop*: Susan stresses a point to Willem as mappers relax after one of the workshops

2.2. *Mapping is not just drawing. It is actually a "phenomenological and existential engagement with place"* This was the crux of Mapping Specialist Rev. C. B. Peter's lecture at the opening workshop

2.3. *Looking closely towards mapping this is what I mean:* Peter moves closer to mappers to emphasize his point

2.4. *What does this theologian know about geography?* Dr. Joseph Wandera listens keenly and critically to the "spatial argument" of his former teacher and the current workshop facilitator, Rev. C. B. Peter

2.5. *The map behind me actually represents the place out there:* Peter was very emphatic about our "phenomenological engagement with place" throughout the mapping workshops.

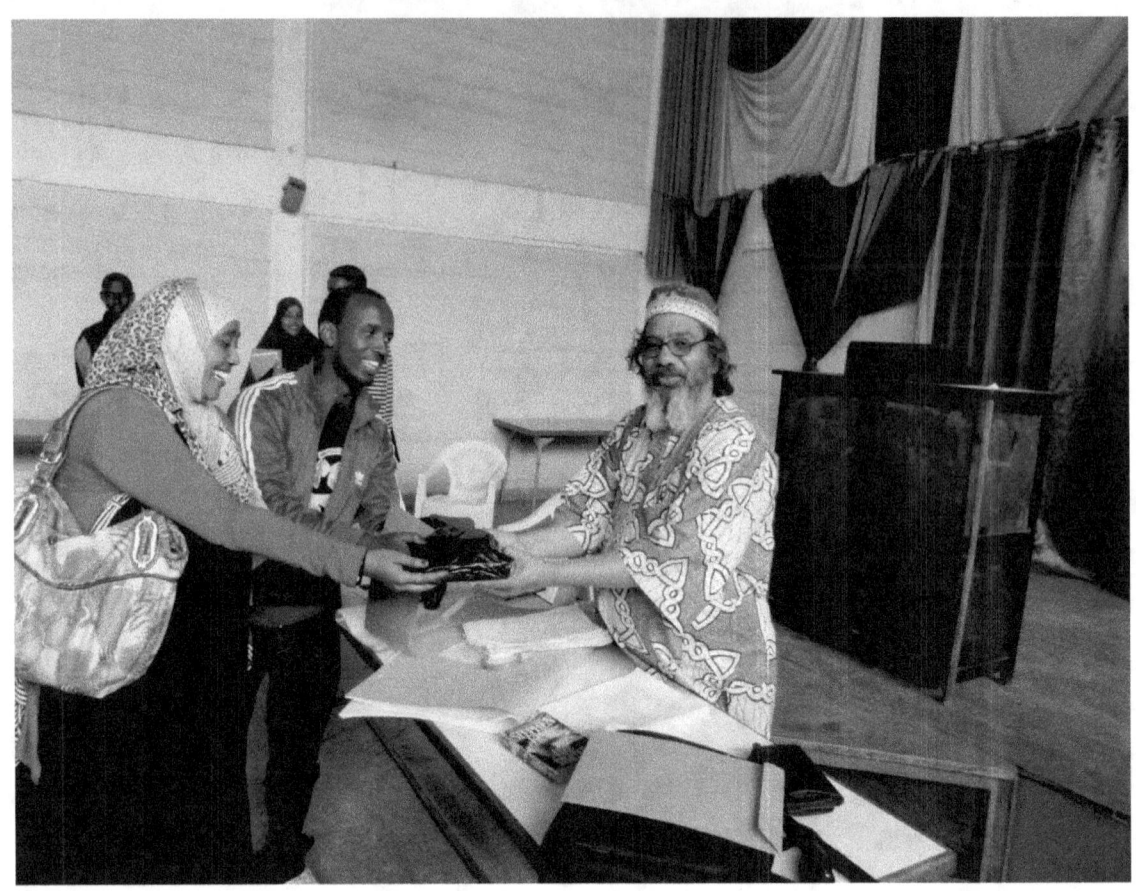

2.6.*A date with the Sheikh:* Mappers Zeituna and Tari present a box of Arabian dates to their mapping mentor, Rev. C. B. Peter, as a mark of their appreciation and gratitude for teaching them the life-transformative skills of mapping

3. Mappers at Work

After the orientation workshop, mappers engaged in a grueling schedule of walking the streets of Eastleigh to record their observations. For this purpose they had been supplied with "Mapping Datasheets". After recording their observations, they returned to base to construct their maps in groups. Finally they presented their maps in a final evaluation workshop which involved a group critique and appraisal of each map.

3.1.*Did I lose my way?* Bernadette Massaquoi observes keenly the sights, sounds, and smells of Street 8 as she maps the place

3.2. *And then, return to the base:* Mappers recapitulate their observations on paper as they draw their maps under the watchful eye of their mentor, Rev. C. B. Peter

3.3. *Her own person:* Mapping helps Jenipher realize that she is her own person as she draws away from the crowd to build her map

3.4.*Outside, inside, outside:* Some mappers finalizing their mapping notes and datasheets before embarking on the exercise of drawing maps

3.5.*And finally, this is our map of Street 1:* Muktar [left] and Ochieng [right] present their map at the evaluation workshop at which all maps were similarly presented by their respective teams and discussed in plenary

4. Eastleigh Maps

Finally, maps are more useful than mere raw data in social surveys. They combine feeling, perception, and empirical findings about places. Looking at various maps portrays the enriching diversity of Eastleigh streets as well as the men and women who mapped them.

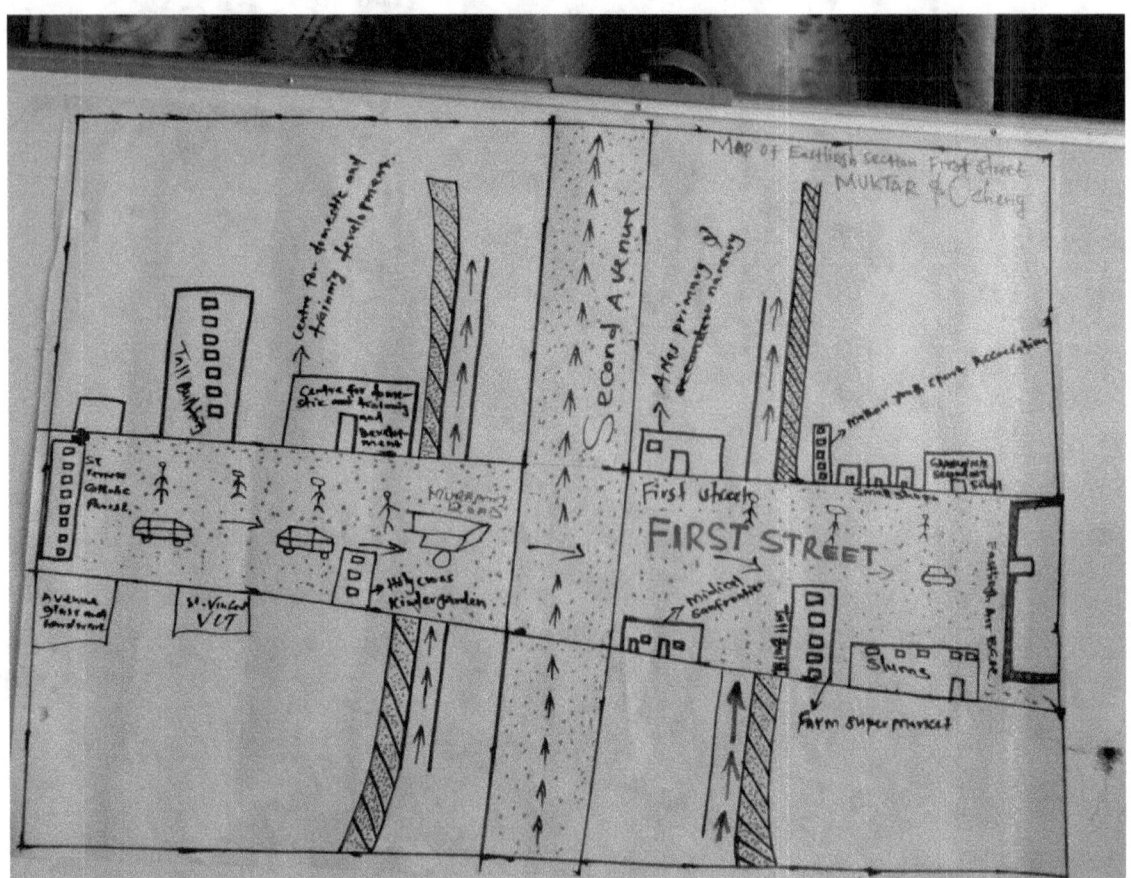

Street 1

Street 2

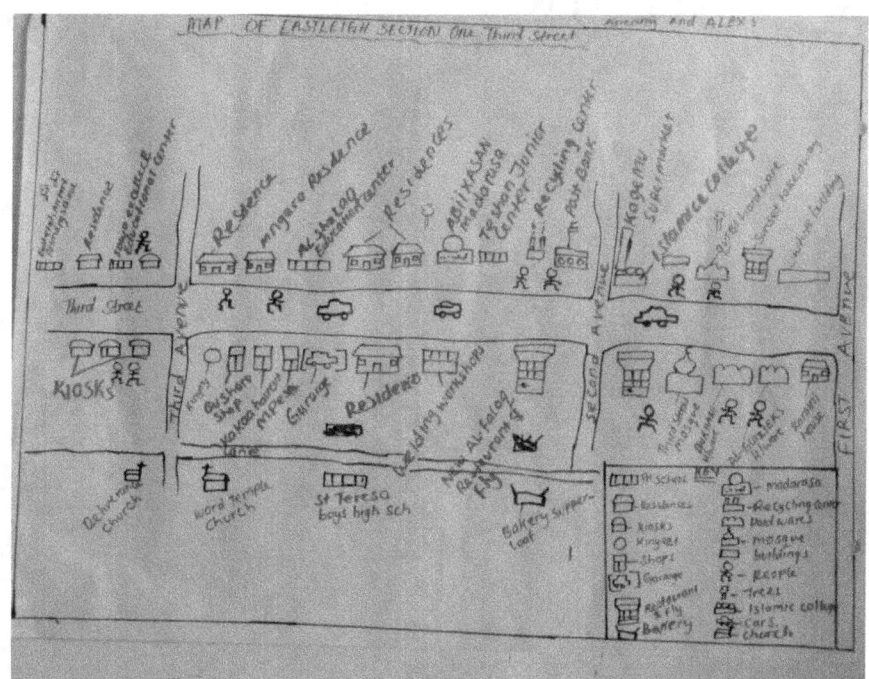

Street 3

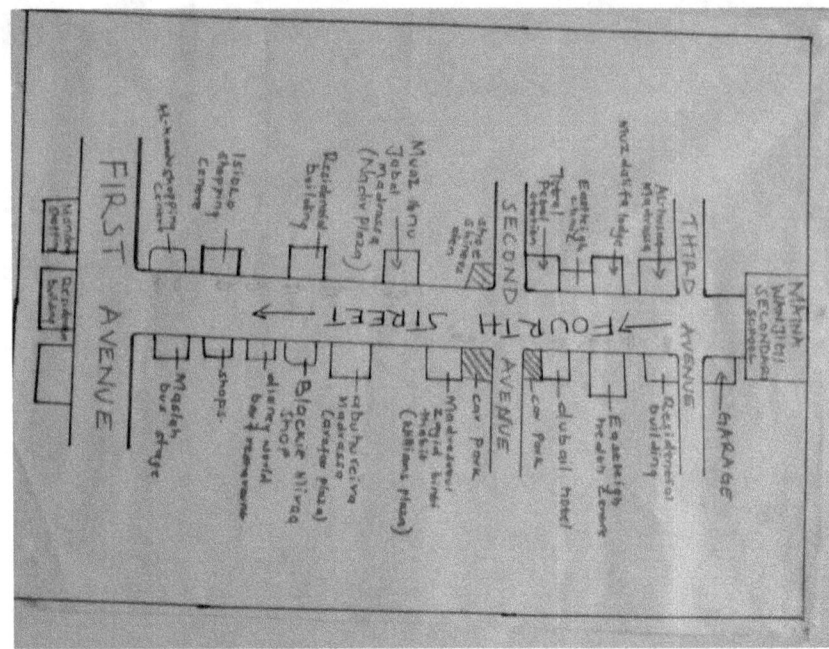

Street 4

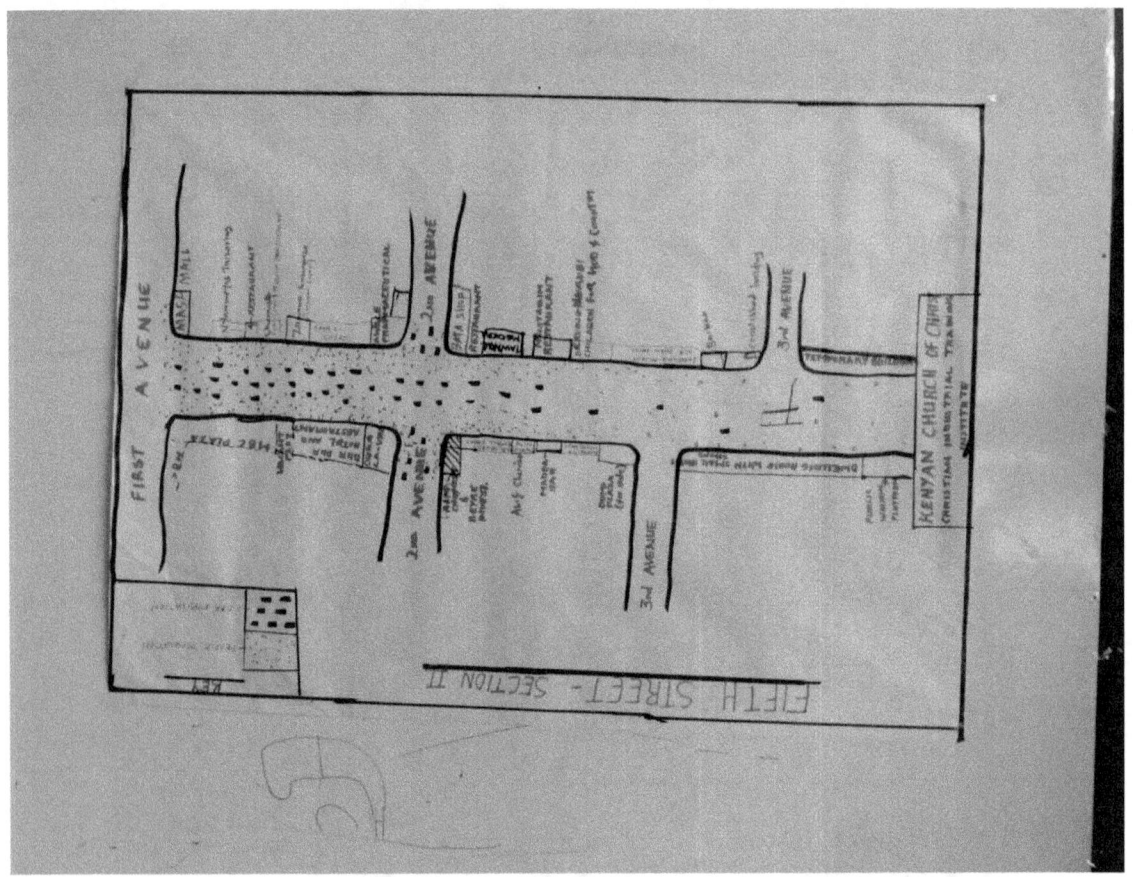

Street 5

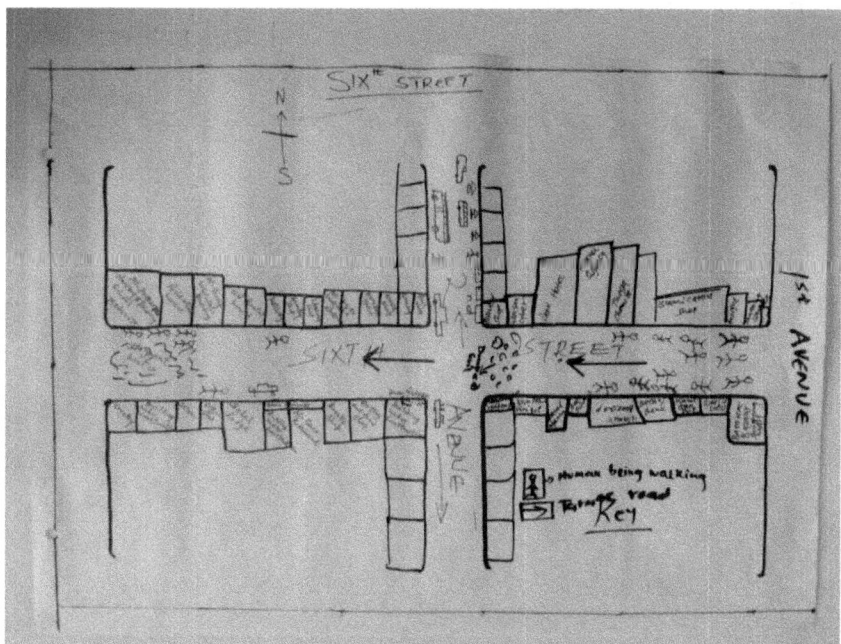

Street 6

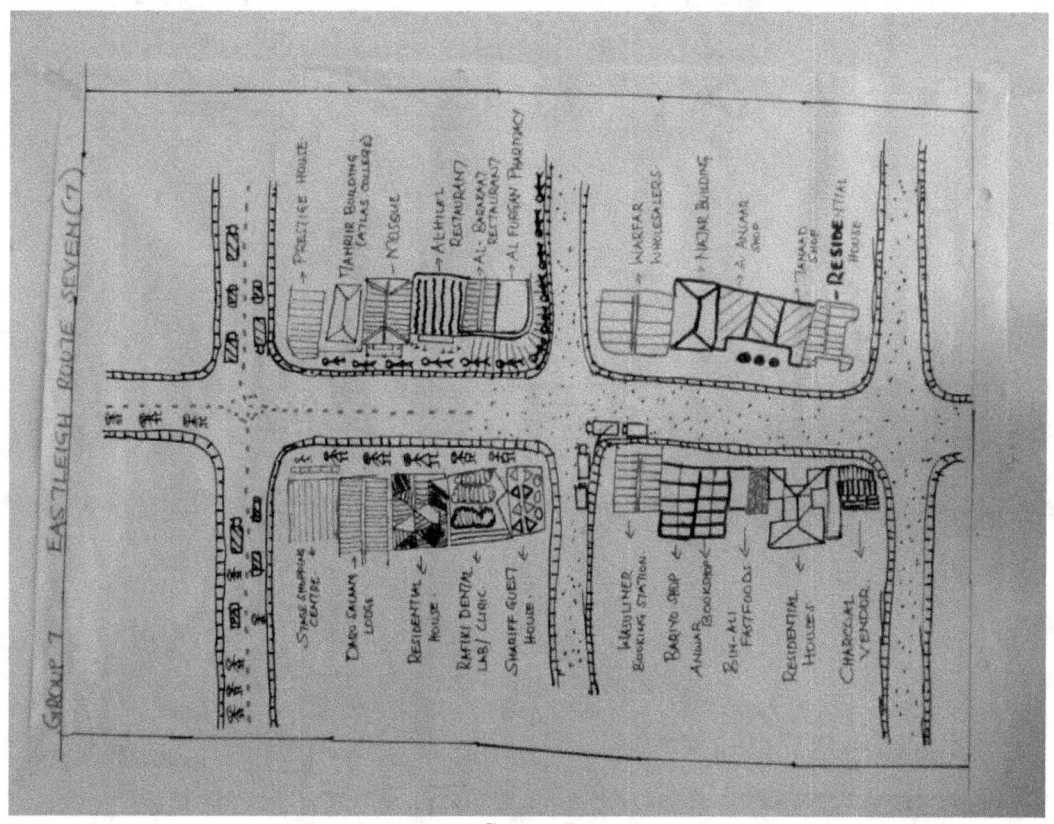

Street 7

Street 8

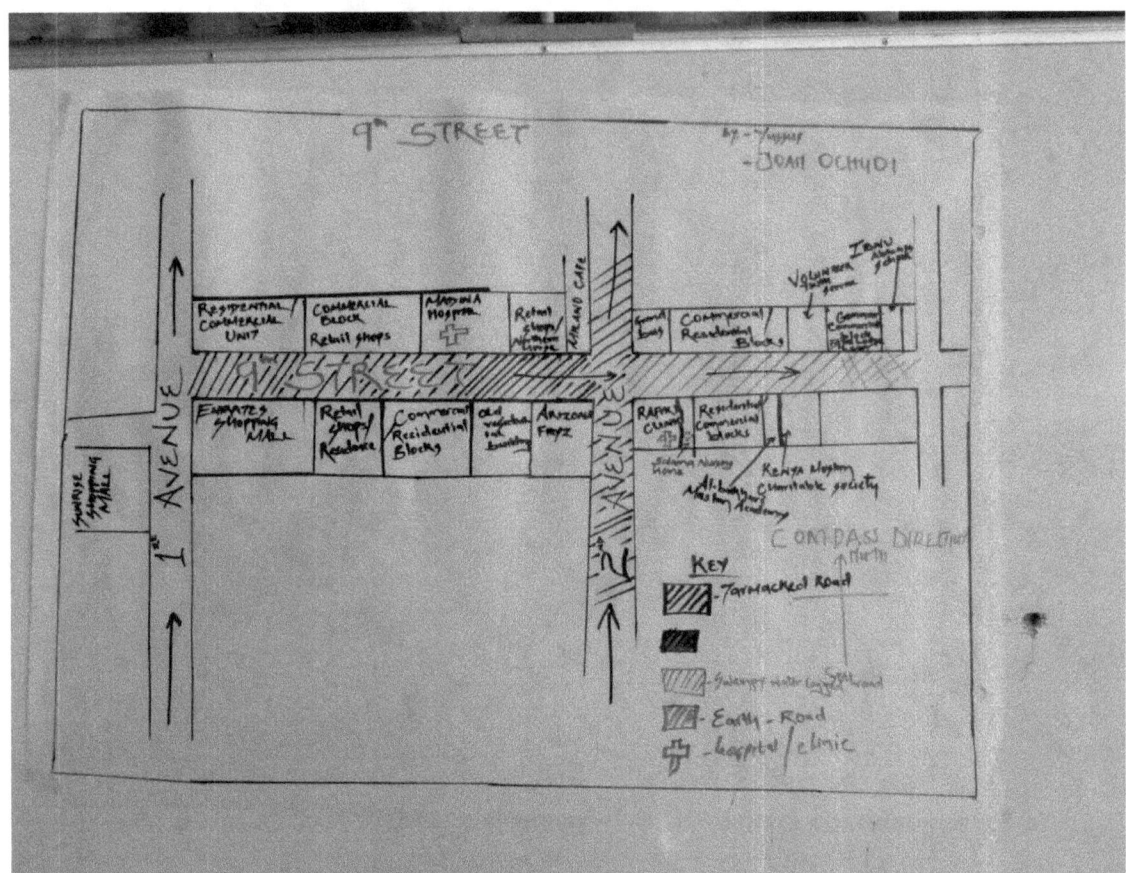

Street 9

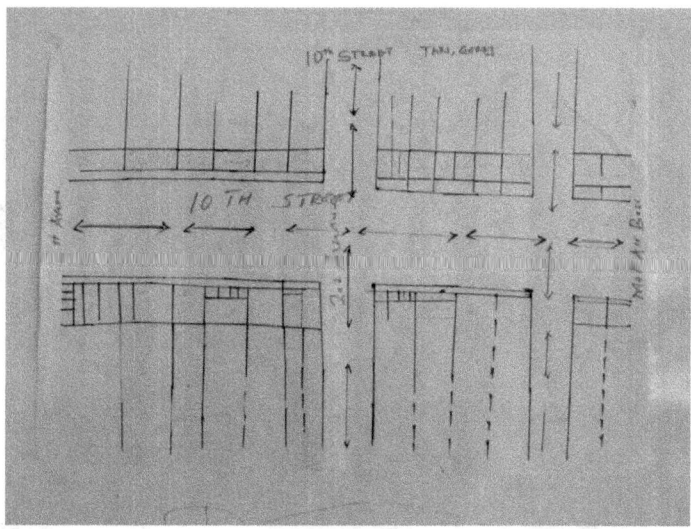

Street 10

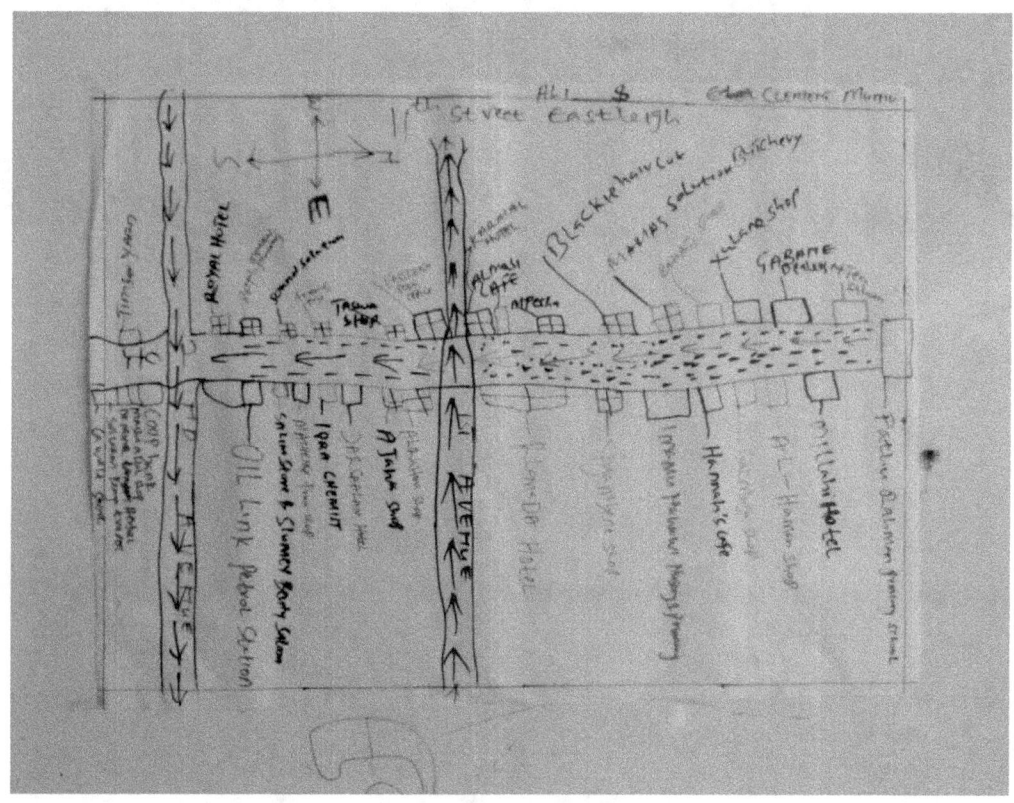

Street 11

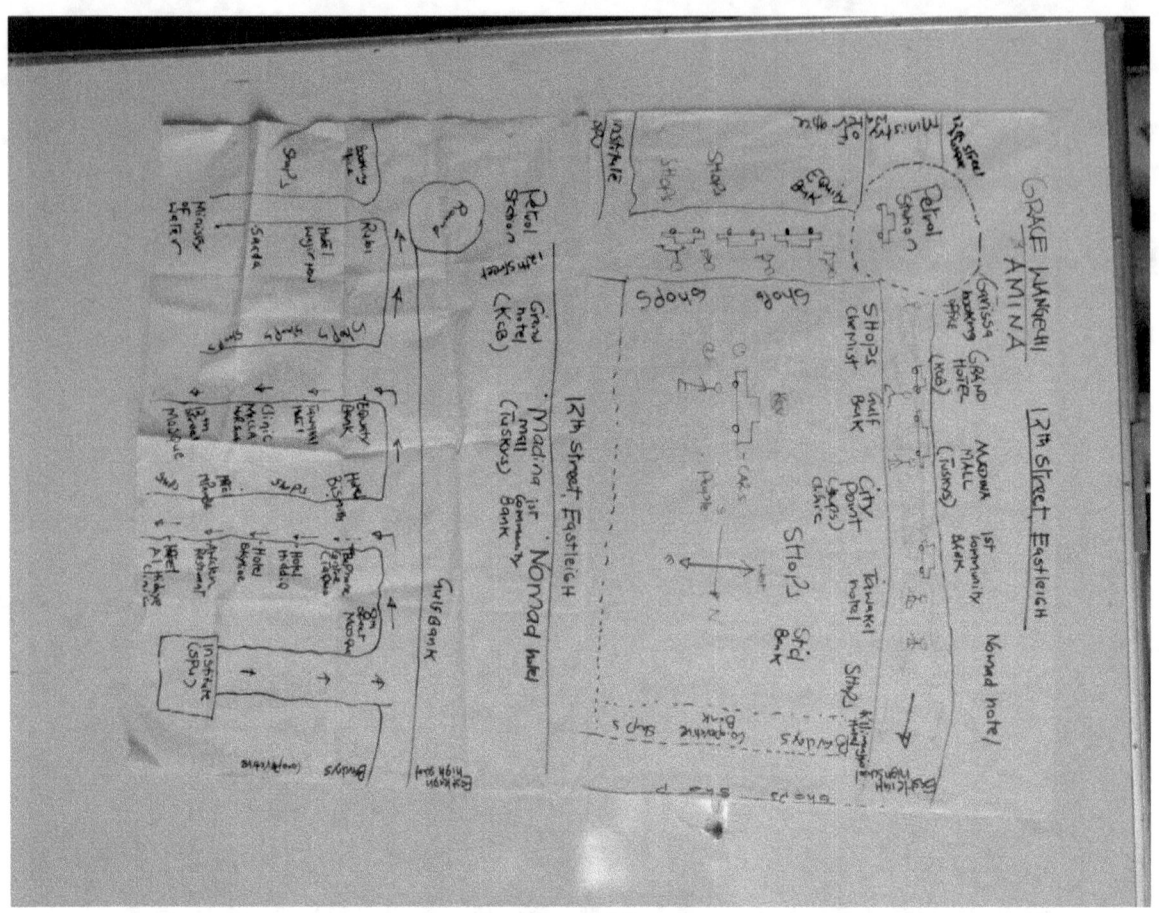

Street 12

APPENDIX 2

List of Contributors

Sufi Merabaqsh Abdulaziz Bunni
Sufi Merabaqsh is a Sufi wise man who has lived in Eastleigh for many years.

Issack Ibrahim
Mr. Isaack Ibrahim, a former Christian, is a Muslim public preacher in Eastleigh.

Willem Jansen
The Rev. Willem J.E Jansen is a lecturer at St. Paul's University, Limuru, Kenya, for the Programme of Islam and Christian-Muslim relations (ICMR), since 2009. He studied Theology at Kampen University and Free University Amsterdam, both in The Netherlands. He studied and worked at Cairo University, Egypt, and at the Christian Study Centre, Rawalpindi, Pakistan. He is a PhD candidate at Tilburg University, The Netherlands. He is a minister of the Protestant Church in The Netherlands.

C. B. Peter
The Rev. C. B. Peter, a senior lecturer in the Faculty of Theology at St. Paul's University is currently writing his PhD thesis on "The Role of Mapping in Theological Reflection: A Cross-Cultural Study" registered at the Trinity Saint David University of Wales, Lampeter (UK).

Joseph Wandera
Dr. Joseph Wandera has recently completed his PhD at the University of Cape Town, South Africa. Joseph, a lecturer in the Department of Islam and Christian-Muslim Relations (ICMR) at St. Paul's University is a co-founder of the Centre for Christian-Muslim Relations in Eastleigh (CCMRE) together with the Rev. Willem Jansen.

Halkano Abdi Wario
Dr. Halkano Abdi Wario, a resident Muslim researcher in Eastleigh, is currently a post doctoral candidate registered under a VW research grant in the University of Beyreuth Germany.

APPENDIX 3

List of Mappers

Eastleigh
1. Amina Ali
2. Liban Nor
3. Hannan Gavad
4. Kaltuma Mohamed
5. Hassan Billow
6. Tari Aden
7. Diba Hassan
8. Wako Yussuf
9. Omar Daud
10. Zeituna Hussein
11. Muktar Adan
12. Alex Ondieki Omboto

St Paul's
1. Antony Mwangi
2. Grace Wangechi
3. Antony Wainaina
4. Susan Olulo
5. Nekesa Lusabe
6. Ochieng Odindo
7. Gerishom Omelo
8. James Waweru
9. Kesho Joseph
10. Clement Muniu
11. Joan Ochudi
12. Bernadette Yema Kadie Massaquioi
13. Adama Faye
14. Phillip Eliah

APPENDIX 4

Letter from the Supreme Council of Kenya Muslim (SUPKEM) Supporting the Eastleigh Mapping Project

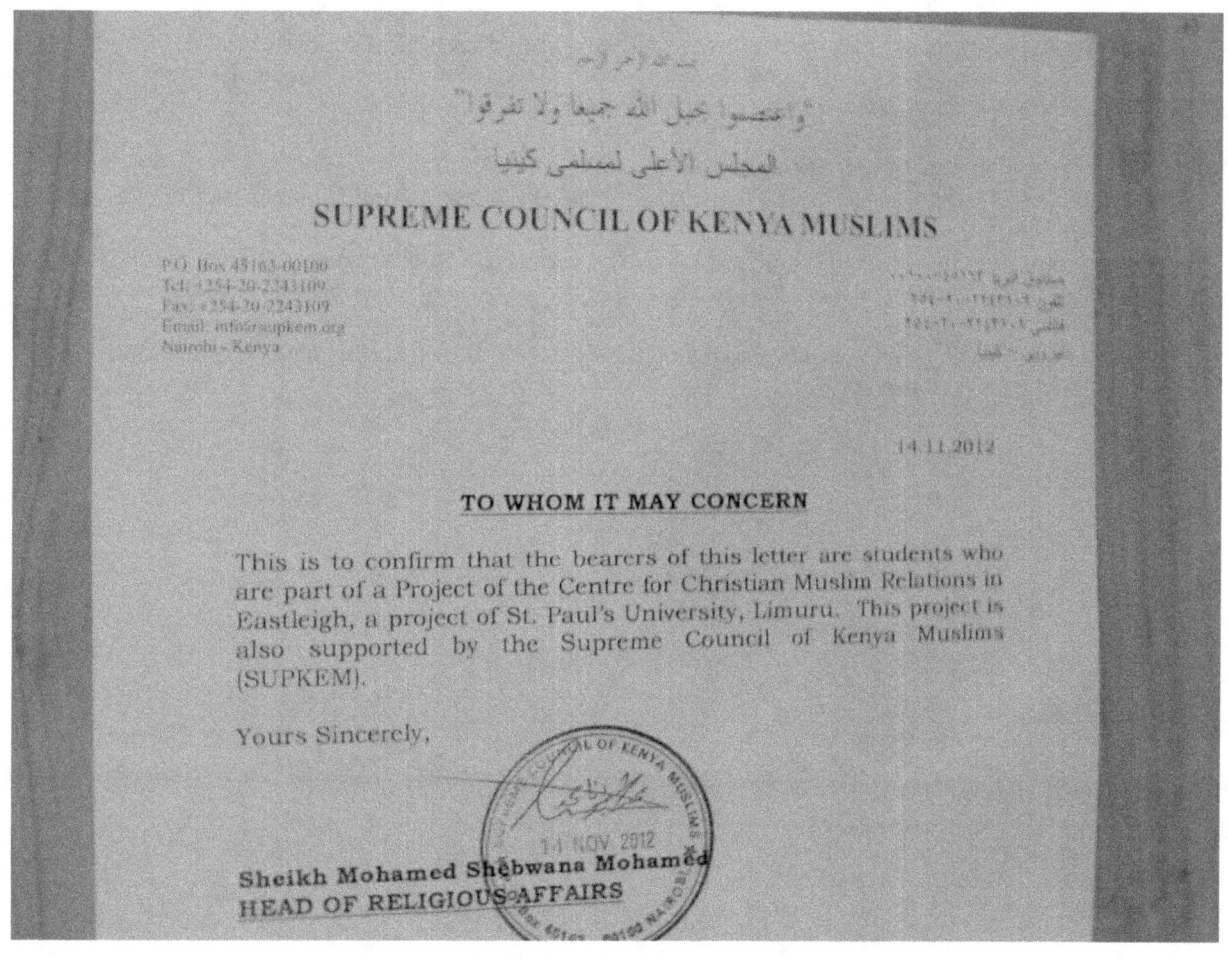

Zapf Chancery Tertiary Level Publications (Continued)

Abortion and Morality Debate in Africa: A Philosophical Enquiry **by George Kegode** (2010)
The Holy Spirit as Liberator: A Study of Luke 4: 14-30 **by Joseph Koech** (2010)
Biblical Studies, Theology, Religion and Philosophy: An Introduction for African Universities, **Gen. Ed. James N. Amanze** (2010)
Modeling for Servant-Leaders in Africa: Lessons from St. Paul **by Ndung'u John Brown Ikenye** (2010)
HIV & AIDS, Communication and Secondary Education in Kenya **by Ndeti Ndati** (2011)
Disability, Society and Theology: Voices from Africa **by Samuel Kabue et al** (2011)
If You Have No Voice Just Sing!: Narratives of Women's Lives and Theological Education at St. Paul's University **by Esther Mombo And Heleen Joziasse** (2011)
Mutira Mission: An African Church Comes of Age in Kirinyaga, Kenya (1912-2012) **by Julius Gathogo** (2011)
The Bible and African Culture: Mapping Transactional Inroads **by Humphrey Waweru** (2011)
Karl Jaspers' Philosophy of Existence: Insights for Out Time **by Cletus N. Chukwu** (2011)
Diet of Worms: Quality of Catering in Kenyan Prisons **by Jacqueline Cheptekkeny Korir** (2011)
Our Father! An Indian Christian Prays the Lord's Prayer **by C. B. Peter** (2011)
African Christianity: The Stranger Within **by Joseph D. Galgalo** (2012)
A Handbook of African Church History **by Medard Rugyendo** (2012)
Project Planning and Management: A Kenyan Experience **by Zablon Bundi Mutongu and Lily Wanjiku Njanja** (2012)
Reading and Comprehension in the African Context: A Cognitive Enquiry **by Agnes Wanja Kibui** (2012)
Researching AIDS, Sexuality, and Gender: Experiences of Women in Kenyan Universities **by Nyokabi Kamau** (2013)
Mapping Eastleigh for Christian-Muslim Relations Edited by **C. B. Peter, Joseph M. Wandera, and Willem J. E. Jansen** (2013)

******

Worldwide Distributors of Zapf Chancery Publications

AFRICAN BOOKS COLLECTIVE (www.africanbookscollective.com)
PO Box 721
Oxford OX1 9EN
UK Tel: +44 (0) 1865 58 9756
Fax: +44 (0) 1865 412 341
US Tel: +1 415 644 5108
Customer Services please email orders@africanbookscollective.com
Marketing and Production Justin Cox
justin.cox@africanbookscollective.com
US Customer Assistance Carolina Bruno carolina.bruno@africanbookscollective.com